T0345227

*What Is Africa to Me?*

•

THE AFRICA LIST

# What Is Africa to Me?

FRAGMENTS OF A TRUE-TO-LIFE
AUTOBIOGRAPHY

MARYSE CONDÉ

*Translated by Richard Philcox*

LONDON NEW YORK CALCUTTA

SERIES EDITOR Rosalind C. Morris

**Seagull Books, 2017**

Original © Éditions Jean-Claude Lattès, 2012

First published in English translation by Seagull Books, 2017

English translation © Richard Philcox, 2017

ISBN 978 0 8574 2 376 4

**British Library Cataloguing-in-Publication Data**
A catalogue record for this book is available
from the British Library.

Typeset by Seagull Books, Calcutta, India
Printed and bound by Maple Press, York, Pennsylvania, USA

*For Hazel Joan Rowley*
*who suddenly slammed the door shut*
*that she had left open for us*

'You must choose between living and writing.'

*Jean-Paul Sartre*

Why is it that any attempt to write about one's life ends up as a jumble of half-truths? Why does it have to be that any autobiography or memoir all too often becomes a construction of fantasies where the simple truth fades, then disappears altogether? Why is it that we are so anxious to depict a life so different from what we have lived? I read, for example, in my publisher's press release on the basis of information I provide for journalists and booksellers: 'In 1958, she married Mamadou Condé, an actor from Guinea, whom she saw perform at the Odeon Theater in *Les Nègres*, a play by Jean Genet, directed by Roger Blin, and left with him for Guinea, the only African country that said "No" to General de Gaulle's referendum.'

The above information conjures up an appealing picture of love enlightened by political commitment. And yet it is far from the truth. I never saw Condé perform in *Les Nègres*. While I was with him in

Paris, he acted in small parts in obscure theatres where he played 'the nigger' as he used to joke. It was only in 1959 that he played Archibald at the Odeon, long after the first of our many separations, since our marriage had been far from a success story. I was teaching at Bingerville in the Ivory Coast where Sylvie-Anne, our first daughter, was born.

Paraphrasing Jean-Jacques Rousseau, therefore, in his *Confessions,* I declare today that 'I propose to show my fellows a woman as Nature made her and this woman shall be me.'

In a manner of fashion, I have always felt passionate about the truth which, both in private and in public, has often been to my detriment. In my childhood memories, *Tales from the Heart: True Stories from My Childhood*, I recount how my 'vocation as a writer' (if we can use such an expression) came about. I must have been around ten. I think it was one 28th April, the birthday of my mother whom I adored but whose singular, complex and capricious character never failed to disconcert me. I had apparently devised a piece that was composed of a poem and a short play where I attempted to act out the various facets of her personality, sometimes tender and serene like a sea breeze, sometimes spiteful and moody. My mother is said to have listened to me without saying a word while I paraded in front of

•

her dressed in a blue frock. Then she looked up at me, her eyes brimming with tears, to my amazement, and sighed: 'So that's how you see me?' At that very moment I felt a surge of power that I have attempted to relive, book after book.

This anecdote fabricated a posteriori seems to me the perfect illustration of those unwitting (?) endeavours of embellishment that I am denouncing. No doubt I have often dreamt of shocking my readers by debunking certain impostures. More than once I have regretted that certain barbs in my texts have gone unnoticed. For instance, in my last novel *En attendant la montée des eaux* (2010), I wrote: 'Isn't a terrorist quite simply an outcast, someone excluded from his land, from wealth and happiness who desperately and perhaps barbarically endeavours to make himself heard?'

I had hoped that, in our overly chary times, such a definition would get some kind of reaction. But only Didier Jacob interviewing me for the *Nouvel Observateur* raised the question.

The desire to shock, however, is not enough to assume the vocation of a writer. I was swept up almost unwittingly by my passion for writing. I shall not compare it to a mysterious malady since it has given me enormous joy. I would rather compare it to a compulsion, somewhat scary, whose cause I have never been able to unravel. Let us not forget that I was born in an island at a time when there was no museum, no real theatre, where the only writers we came across were in our school textbooks and who originated Elsewhere.

I did not become a writer at an early age, scribbling extraordinary texts at the age of sixteen. My first novel was published when I was forty-two, when other writers have begun to put away their pens and paper, and was received very badly, which I stoically believed to be a premonition of my future literary career. The main reason for writing so late was that I had until then been so occupied with the tribulations of life that I had no time for anything else. In fact, I began to write only when my life got less problematic and I was able to trade my real-life dramas for paper ones.

I have described in detail the background I came from in *Tales from the Heart* and especially in *Victoire, My Mother's Mother*. Euzhan Palcy's hit film *Sugar Cane Alley* popularized a certain image of the French Antilles. No, not all of us belong to the wretched of the earth, working ourselves to death amid the sting of the sugar cane. My parents belonged to the embryo of a middle class and called themselves, presumptuously, 'Les Grands Nègres'. It must be said in their defence that their childhood had been terrible and so they wanted to protect their children at all costs. Jeanne Quidal, my mother, was the illegitimate daughter of an illiterate mulatto woman, Victoire, who couldn't speak a word of French. Victoire hired her services out to a family of white Creoles, the Wachters, and very early on experienced

•

her share of shame and humiliation. Auguste Boucolon, my father, was also an illegitimate child, orphaned when his poor mother was burnt alive as her shack went up in flames. Nevertheless, we can safely say that these painful circumstances had relatively positive results. The Wachters authorized my mother to benefit from their son's private tutor; hence, 'abnormally' educated given her colour, she became one of her generation's first black elementary-school teachers. My father, a ward of the local authorities, pursued his education, unusual for the time, with the help of scholarships and ended up founding a small local bank, the Caisse Coopérative de Prêts, for government officials.

Once they were married, Jeanne and Auguste were the first black couple to own a car, a Citroën C4, to build a two-storey house in Pointe-à-Pitre and to spend their vacations in their 'change of air' house on the banks of the Sarcelles in Goyave. Steeped in self-importance, they considered nothing good enough for them, and raised us, my seven brothers and sisters as well as me, in contempt and ignorance of the society around us. As the last of seven siblings, I was particularly spoilt. Everybody agreed that I would have an exceptional career, and I believed them. At the age of sixteen, when I left for university in Paris, I could not speak a word of Creole. Never having attended a *lewoz* dance, I had no knowledge of the traditional *gwoka* rhythms. For me, even the cuisine from the French Antilles was crude and unrefined.

In the pages that follow, I shall not talk about my present life, devoid of drama, except for illness and old age creeping up on me, which, I'm sure, will not interest anybody. I shall try, rather, to figure out the considerable role Africa has played in my life and imagination. What was I looking for? I still don't know for sure. At the end of the day, I wonder whether the words of Marcel Proust's hero in *Swann in Love* are not appropriate for my time in Africa: 'To think that I ruined years of my life, that I wanted to die, and that the love of my life was for a woman who was neither to my taste nor to my liking.'

I

*Better a Bad Marriage than Staying Single*
Guadeloupean Proverb

I got to know Mamadou Condé in 1958 at the hostel for West African students, a large dilapidated building situated on the boulevard Poniatowski in Paris. Since I considered Africa, its past and its present, my sole preoccupation, I had just met two sisters, Fulanis from Guinea, Ramatoulaye and Binetou, at a political meeting at the Sociétés Savantes, which no longer exists, on the rue Danton. They came from Labbé and made me dream of Africa by showing me the sepia photos of their venerable parents, dressed in rich damask boubous, sitting in front of their round huts with straw roofs.

The student hostel was filled with draughts. As a way of beating the cold, Ramatoulaye, Binetou and I used to drink cups and cups of mint tea in the entrance hall where a tiny coal stove burnt.

·

One afternoon, a group of Guineans joined us. They all referred to Condé as 'Le Vieux' (old man) which, I learnt later, was a mark of respect, but also because with his greying hair he seemed older than the average student. He also spoke with the sententious voice of a sage as if expressing the undeniable truth. His birth certificate, however, stated that he was born around 1930 and thus contradicted both his appearance and behaviour. Easily feeling the cold, he wore a heavy hand-knitted scarf and, under his thick, mud-coloured coat, two or three pullovers. I was surprised when the introductions were made. An actor enrolled in classes at the Conservatoire on the rue Blanche? His diction left much to be desired. As for his high-pitched voice, there was nothing of a baritone about it. Let's be frank. In other times, I would have barely spoken to him. But my life had been radically transformed. I was no longer the person I once was. The once-arrogant Maryse Boucolon, descendant of the Grands Nègres, raised with the utmost contempt for one's inferiors, had been mortally wounded. Fleeing my former friends, all I wanted to do was keep a low profile. I had left the Lycée Fénelon, and I no longer boasted of being one of the few Antilleans preparing for the competitive entrance exams to the Grandes Ecoles with a good chance of being admitted. And that was not my only claim to fame! After Fanon's *Black Skin, White Masks* was published in the journal *L'Esprit*, in a fit of rage at this degrading depiction of Antillean society, I sent an open letter to the editor stating that, in my opinion, Fanon had understood absolutely nothing about the French Antilles. To my great surprise, by way of a response to my impassioned missive, despite my young years, I was invited by Jean-Marie Domenach, no less, to the offices on the rue Jacob, to explain myself.

Since those days of splendour, however, the Haitian Jean Dominique, the future hero of *The Agronomist*, the hagiographical documentary by American director Jonathan Demme, had passed through my life.

I don't recall the exact circumstances in which I met the man who was to have such an impact on my life. We were intensely involved in a remarkable intellectual love. Given the splendid isolation in which I had been brought up, I knew nothing about the history of Haiti. Jean Dominique not only taught me a thing or two physically, he also enlightened me by introducing me to the exploits of the 'brocaded Africans', as Bonaparte scornfully described the Haitians. Thanks to him, I discovered the martyrdom of Toussaint Louverture, the triumph of Jean-Jacques Dessalines and the initial difficulties of the new black republic. He also made me read *Masters of the Dew* by Jacques Roumain, *Bon Dieu rit* by Edris Saint-Amand and *General Sun, My Brother* by Jacques Stephen Alexis. In short, he introduced me to the extraordinary wealth of a land I knew nothing about. Without a doubt it is he who planted in my heart my unfailing attachment to Haiti.

The day I plucked up courage to tell him I was pregnant, he seemed happy, very happy even, and cried out in joy: 'This time it'll be a little mulatto boy!' since he had two girls from a previous union, one of whom, J. J. Dominique, has become a writer.

But when I arrived at his place the following morning, I found him emptying his flat and packing his bags. He solemnly explained that a major threat was looming over Haiti. A physician by the name of François Duvalier was a candidate for the presidential elections. Because he was black, he was drawing enthusiastic crowds who were tired of mulatto presidents and dangerously attracted to his ideology of Noirisme, the Haitian brand of Negritude. He had none of the qualifications necessary to become president and therefore the opposition had to join forces against this loathsome prospect.

Jean Dominique flew off and never even sent me a postcard. I remained alone in Paris, abandoned during my pregnancy. It was unbelievable. I refused to accept the only possible explanation—my colour. As a mulatto, Jean Dominique had treated me with the contempt and thoughtlessness of the so-called elite. How otherwise could I interpret his anti-Duvalier position? How credible was his faith in the people? For me, naturally, it was pure hypocrisy.

The long months of this solitary pregnancy were unbearable. Since one of the physicians in charge of the students found me to be depressive and under-nourished, he sent me to a convalescent home in the

Oise. I shall never forget the kindness showered on me there. For the first time I discovered the kindness of strangers. Finally, on 13 March 1956, when I should have been preparing for the competitive exam for the Ecole Normale Supérieure, I gave birth in a small clinic in the fifteenth arrondissement to a boy whom I randomly named Denis. Around that time, my beloved mother suddenly died in Guadeloupe. In the grip of these ordeals, I was transformed into a Marguerite Gautier. Detecting tuberculosis in my right lung, the same physician sent me to a sanatorium in Vence in the South of France. I was to stay there for over a year.

'Why is fate treating you so badly?' Yvane Randal, one of the few friends I had left, kept saying in dismay as she accompanied me to the train station.

I was so wrapped up in my grief that I didn't even hear her. Since I had very little money, I had to entrust my adorable baby to child welfare, housed in an austere building on the avenue Denfert Rochereau. And yet I had two older sisters living in Paris: Ena, my godmother, extraordinarily beautiful, melancholic and dreamy, wrapped in an aura of mystery. She had come to study music, and, just before the Second World War, married Guadeloupean Guy Tirolien. A graduate of the National School of Administration, he later became our poet laureate with his collection *Balles d'Or*. The reason for their divorce was one of our family's unspeakable secrets.

•

While her husband languished in a Nazi concentration camp alongside Léopold Sedar Senghor, she cheated on him with a clique of dashing German soldiers who nicknamed her 'jewel'. At the time of our story, she was the mistress of a wealthy businessman. In order to pass the time, she would play Chopin on her piano and drink hard liquor. The other sister, Gillette, was more down to earth. She was a social worker in Saint-Denis, at the time a poor, crowded suburb of Paris; she was married to Jean Deen, a medical student from Guinea.

'You don't deserve this!' Yvane said, disgusted.

I did not know what to think. Sometimes I was convinced I was the victim of an enormous injustice. At other times a voice whispered that I had got what I deserved, since the conviction of being raised as a superior human had irritated the Fates. I emerged from this experience a tormented soul, trusting little to fate and dreading at every moment Destiny's double dealing.

The sojourn in Vence turned out to be grim. Like Marie-Noelle in my novel *Desirada*, I have gloomy memories of long hours in bed, daily perfusions, fatigue, nausea, fever, night sweats and insomnia. But unlike Marie-Noelle I did not fall in love. That would have been difficult. Whenever we were feeling better, we were allowed an outing to Nice; once a month and under the guidance of a white-coated nurse. Passers-by stepped aside at our approach, since we symbolized affliction and sickness, and those, as we

know, are contagious. We would walk down to the
seafront and cast envious eyes at the tanned and
healthy half-naked men swimming the breast stroke
and racing one another. I grieved at the thought of
my beautiful baby and of my mother whom I would
never see again while still hating Jean Dominique.
Nevertheless, as often happens in life, these long
months had a fortunate recompense. Thanks to a
series of special allowances due to my condition, I
was able to finish my degree in modern languages
from the university at Aix-en-Provence. I opted for
French, English and Italian and not French, Latin
and Greek, as I had planned when in my senior
preparatory class at the lycée.

Back in Paris I found work from a classified ad at a
branch of the Ministry for Culture, rue Boissy
d'Anglas. Thanks to this job, I believed I could look
after Denis again and put a stop to the guilty feelings
I had whenever I thought of him. But, very quickly,
my life turned out to be a living hell. Since the death
of my mother, my father, who had never shown me
much affection anyway, completely lost interest in
me and stopped sending me any money. I never
understood why Ena's and Gillette's attitude towards
me changed as well. Both considerably older, we had
never been very close. Yet in the past they had been
rather kind, often inviting me to lunch or dinner.
Since my pregnancy and Jean Dominique's flight,
they were no longer to be seen—at a time when I

needed them the most. Whenever I ventured to call them, they would all but hang up when they heard my voice. Had I shocked their petty-bourgeois feelings? Were they disappointed at seeing me pregnant and abandoned like a common servant whereas I was the one who had been destined for a brilliant future?

My baby and I therefore had only my paltry wage from the Ministry for Culture to live on. As coincidence would have it, I lived in a plush block of flats opposite the Haitian Embassy in the seventeenth arrondissement, but in a maid's room with the WC on the landing. Every morning I would travel across Paris to leave Denis at the students' day-care centre on the rue des Fossés Saint Jacques in the fifth arrondissement, then dash to the Ministry near the Place de la Concorde. At the end of the day, I travelled the same distance back. As you can guess, I never went out for an evening. Once so fond of the movies, the theatre, of concerts and dining out, I no longer went anywhere. I ran my son his bath, gave him dinner, then sang him lullabies and tried to get him to fall asleep. Since it was rumoured that my sudden disappearance was due to my being an 'unmarried mother'—single mothers were treated with scorn at the time, except by the loyal Yvane Randal and Eddie Edinval—the Antillean students avoided me. I kept company solely with the Africans who knew nothing about me and who were impressed by my manners and what was left of my way with words.

I had great trouble paying the rent. When it was long overdue, the landlord, a picture-postcard bourgeois with snowy white hair and an aristocratic profile, would climb the six floors to the poky little hole he had rented me, and shout: 'I'm not your father, you know!'

At the Ministry, however, I rediscovered those gestures of kindness and thoughtfulness that had so delighted me during my stay at the convalescent home in the Oise. In the words of Tennessee Williams, I was constantly surrounded by the kindness of strangers. The department where I worked took pity on my youth and destitution and admired my dignity and courage. On weekends I was invited to lunch by my colleagues. The guests would go into raptures over Denis, shower him with kisses and treat him like a little prince. As I would prepare to leave, my hostesses would slip into my bag an assortment of second-hand clothes, and not only for the baby, as well as packets of gingerbread, cans of Ovalmaltine and Van Houten cocoa, designed to strengthen mother and son, since both of us were somewhat puny.

I would shed tears of humiliation outside on the pavement.

What did we do at the Ministry on the rue Boissy d'Anglas? If I remember correctly, my department drew up letters describing the cultural projects intended for the minister.

•

After a few months I realized that I was in no state to continue such a life. Once again I reluctantly parted with Denis, entrusting him to a certified nurse, Madame Bonenfant, who lived in the vicinity of Chartres. As I was soon incapable of paying her the monthly 18,000 francs, I made myself scarce and never set foot in Chartres again. Madame Bonenfant did not resort to legal proceedings, however, and was content to send me letters, stuffed with spelling mistakes and news of 'our little one'.

'He misses you a lot!' she used to write. 'He asks for you all the time.'

I used to weep as I read her letters for I was racked with remorse. My days went by in a fog of suffering and bad conscience. I slept two or three hours a night. Within a few weeks, I had lost eight kilos. Readers often ask me why my novels are filled with mothers who consider their children a heavy cross to bear, and children who suffer from not being loved and withdraw into themselves. Because I write from experience. I loved my son very deeply. But not only did his presence wreck the prospects for which my education had destined me, I was also incapable of raising him. In the end, my behaviour towards him did seem like that of a heartless mother.

I have no memory whatsoever of Condé's headlong rush into courtship: neither a first kiss, nor a first embrace nor a shared moment of sexual pleasure. Nothing. Nor do I remember any conversation, literary or political, of a serious nature. For different reasons, we were both in a hurry to get married: I was hoping to restore my status in society; Condé to exhibit a wife with a university degree, from a good family and speaking French like a true Parisian. He was a somewhat complex character, gifted with a cheeky humour that I often found common, almost vulgar, but effective. I endeavoured in vain to fashion him to my taste, but he repelled my various attempts with a determination which testified to his independence of mind. Once I wanted him to wear a parka which was very much in vogue at the time. 'Too young! Much too young for me!' was the reply in that nasal tone of his.

I tried to convey to him my passion for the New Wave filmmakers, for directors such as Antonioni, Fellini and Visconti, for Dreyer and Bergman. But he fell asleep during the screening of Truffaut's *400 Blows* (1958); I had great difficulty waking him up, much to the amusement of those around us. My most bitter failure was when I tried to initiate him to the Negritude poets whom I had discovered a few years previously as a senior preparatory student. One day, Françoise, a classmate who liked to think of herself as a political activist, showed me a slim little book entitled *Discourse on Colonialism*. I had never heard of the author. And yet I was so shaken by what I read that the very next day I went to the bookshop

Présence Africaine and bought everything I could find by Aimé Césaire. For good measure I also bought the poems by Léopold Sédar Senghor and Léon-Gontran Damas.

Condé opened at random *Notebook of a Return to My Native Land* by Césaire, now my favourite author, and read mockingly:

'That 2 and 2 make 5
That the forest meows
That the tree plucks the maroons from the
fire
That the sky strokes its beard
Etc. . . . etc. . . . '

'What does that mean?' he exclaimed. 'Who is he writing for? Certainly not for me. I don't understand a word.'

At a pinch, he tolerated Léon-Gontran Damas whose style he deemed simpler and more direct.

It seems incredible to me now that I never revealed to him the existence of Denis. I wasn't even tempted to, since I knew that such a revelation would annul any wedding plans. Things were very different at that time. Although a woman's virginity was no longer indispensable, the sexual revolution had barely started. It took another fifteen years for Simone Veil's law allowing abortions to be voted in. It wasn't easy confessing to an illegitimate child.

Condé did not get unanimous approval from the few people I introduced him to.

'What's his level of education?' Jean, Gillette's husband, asked when I took Condé to lunch in Saint-Denis.

Ena briefly met us in a bar on the Place des Abbesses and called Gillette to tell her that in half an hour he had downed six beers and two glasses of red wine. He was no doubt a drunkard.

'You can't understand him when he speaks,' Yvane and Eddie complained.

I too could clearly see that he was not the man I had dreamt of. But the man I had dreamt of had betrayed me in a despicable way. We were married one morning in August 1958, under brilliant sunshine, at the city hall of the eighteenth arrondissement. The plane trees were in leaf. Although Ena did not come, Gillette did and attended the ceremony with her daughter Dominique (who sulked because it didn't look like 'a real wedding'). We drank a glass of red Cinzano at the cafe on the corner, then moved into a two-room furnished accommodation that Condé had rented in the neighbourhood.

Less than three months later we were separated. We hadn't quarrelled. We just couldn't bear to be together for any length of time. Everything one of us did or said irritated the other. Sometimes, to act as a buffer, we would invite friends over, but I loathed his acquaintances as much as he detested Yvane and Eddie. When I realized I was pregnant the following year, we made several attempts to get back together. But we had to resign ourselves to breaking up. And

I stoically took in stride what looked like another set-back in my love life. In a certain respect, I had obtained what I wanted—I was now a married woman with a wedding band on my left hand. In a certain respect, the marriage had put my shame to rest. Jean Dominique had imbued me with the fear and distrust of Caribbean men. Condé was an 'African'. Not a 'Guinean' as I later claimed, falsely implying that Sékou Touré and the independence of 1958 had played a capital role in our marriage. At the time, I was not yet sufficiently politicized for that. I believed that if I could reach the continent sung by my favourite poet, I could be reborn. Restore my virginity. Regain my hopes. Erase the malicious memory of the man who had hurt me so much. It was not surprising that my marriage didn't last—I had laid on Condé's shoulders the full burden of expectation and imagination born out of my disillusions. The weight was too heavy for him.

I now see with a cruel lucidity to what extent my marriage to Condé was in fact a fool's bargain. Love and desire had very little to do with it, for he was using me for what he cruelly lacked: an education, and the sense of belonging to a solid family environment. Gillette's husband was right to enquire about his level of education. All he had was his elementary-school certificate. His father had died when he'd been very young, and he'd been brought up in Siguiri by a wretch of a mother who sold trinkets at the market. He was to discover that the role of actor he had chosen with no genuine vocation and only to leave Guinea and assume the handsome role of 'student' had little prestige. Benefiting from no support or connections, his ambitions of 'being somebody', as Marlon Brando said in *On the Waterfront*, had no chance of success.

In 1959, France's overseas development agency began operations. A wing of the ministry soon housed a recruitment office for French citizens who wanted to try their luck in Africa. I went straight for it. The Africa I had discovered in preparatory class was nothing more than a literary object, the source of inspiration for poets whose voice was a change from the usual Rimbaud, Verlaine, Mallarmé and Valéry. Yet, gradually, Africa as a reality loomed larger and larger in my life. I wanted to forget about the Antilles—it had too many painful memories. So I made a dash for the recruitment office.

I remember the amazement on the face of the pink-cheeked fair-haired man who took charge of my application and how he bombarded me with questions: 'You want to go to Africa on your own with a baby? And what about your husband? Haven't you just got married?'

## One Flew over the Cuckoo's Nest

*Milos Forman*

A few months later I received a registered letter informing me that the Ministry of Education had appointed me to the college in Bingerville, Ivory Coast. Given the insufficiency of my diplomas at that time—a degree in modern languages—I was recruited as a teaching assistant in French on the scale of IV and offered a modest salary. It didn't matter. I danced for joy—something I hadn't done in ages.

During the final days of September 1959, Denis and I took the train to the port of Marseille where the steamship *Jean Mermoz* was waiting to take us to Abidjan. Condé had tried to dissuade me from leaving, given my condition. But living with a baby in a foreign land, and giving birth to another without a father, no longer frightened me. As for my sisters, they welcomed the news with a kind of relief, for from now on I would make a fool of myself elsewhere.

•

Far away from them. Gillette hastily invited me to dinner and told me that since Jean had finished his medical studies, she was getting ready to leave for Guinea.

Marseille for me was a powerful literary image, the background of *Banjo*, the book by Jamaican Claude McKay that had inspired a literary cult and garnered praise from an enthusiastic Césaire. Roaming the Canebière, its main thoroughfare, ambling along its crowded streets and sitting in its cafes, I felt as though I was in touch with the writers of the Negritude movement. More importantly, the blood flowed through my veins with renewed elation. A painful digression had closed, and all that remained of my past was a small boy on the edge of tears who could not understand why he had been snatched from the arms of his beloved nurse. The separation from Madame Bonenfant had not been easy. In her generosity, she had endeavoured to play the role of mother to Denis, something nobody had ever done. Things would have been different, she'd mumbled, if I had left for Africa arm in arm with my husband. What on earth was I going to do without a man at my side? Had I thought of the terrible dangers that were lying in wait for me? She made the mistake of listing them: rape, disease . . . and I quickly put her words down to racism.

My voyage to Abidjan could be jokingly compared to Buddha's first outing, when he witnessed poverty, sickness, old age and death. Until then, I had only experienced the world of privilege, a limited world. My many visits to Italy, Spain and the Netherlands comprised visits to the museums. London too had been for the museums and to learn English. Except perhaps for the trip to Warsaw with Jean Dominique: he had dragged me to a youth festival in an attempt to introduce me to the achievements of Marxism and to admire the countries of Eastern Europe. I must confess it was an extraordinary experience. For the first time in my life, I had rubbed shoulders with Indians, Chinese, Japanese and Mongols, and been dazzled by a performance of the Peking Opera.

Since the French administration had been far from generous, I occupied a minute, airless, third-class cabin. But there were some who were worse off, and I could see them from our promenade deck— mostly white or native soldiers, hemmed in like prisoners by a thick wire fence. Numb with cold, they huddled around the braziers lit by the sailors and waited for the soup that was ladled out to them twice a day.

We arrived at Dakar, our first port of call, in the early morning. The sky was milky white above the city. At that time, the capital of French West Africa was a small, peaceful conglomeration, fragrant with flowers, its pretty wooden houses seldom higher than a storey. I remember the strange, penetrating musty smell at the wharf—the smell of groundnuts, floating in the air, thickening it with curls of reddish dust. A member of the crew explained that it was swept in by a burning wind from the desert.

My first sight of Africa certainly did not result in love. Unlike the raptures expressed by Western travellers, I remained oblivious to its scents and colours. And I was overcome by the poverty. Seated on the pavements, women with haggard faces put their twins, their triplets and their quadruplets on display. Legless cripples dragged themselves along on their behinds. The armless brandished their stumps. All kinds of invalids and beggars, wildly shaking their bowls, formed a menacing crowd.

In perfect contrast, the Whites were dashing and well dressed at the wheel of their cars.

Rounding a corner I came across a filthy market. A pestilential smell pervaded the air. Clouds of flies buzzed over colourless fish and joints of purplish meat oozing blood. I ran as fast as I could, until I arrived at a residential neighbourhood. A hubbub of children's voices wafted out of some open windows. A school! Standing on tiptoe, I could see rows of blond heads and next to the blackboard the teacher, also blond, wearing an elegant blue dress.

Where were the little Africans?

Yvane had given me the address of one of her uncles, Jean Sulpice, 'Uncle Jean', a military physician who lived in the French quarter. The family seldom saw any Guadeloupeans but welcomed us with open arms as if we were close relatives, and served us an incredible traditional meal: black sausage, avocado and saltfish, courtbouillon of sea bream, rice and red beans. 'Just like home,' Madame Sulpice proudly asserted.

The atmosphere, however, was somewhat depressing. The entire household was focused on Béatrice, one of the daughters, aged about twelve, who was severely disabled. Claire, one of her sisters, who obviously adored her, fed her with a spoon but she threw up practically everything she swallowed. Getting the better of my unintentional disgust, I went up and stroked her beautiful, soft hands resting palm upwards on her knees.

Uncle Jean, a smiling, tanned mulatto, arrived for dessert. And tried to explain to me what it was like for an Antillean to live in Africa.

It wasn't at all what I'd been expecting.

'The Africans hate and despise us,' he said. 'Because some of us have served as colonial civil servants, they treat us like lackeys only good enough for doing the master's dirty work.'

'But what about René Maran?' I said, outraged.

'Who is René Maran?' he asked, puzzled.

At first I thought I had misheard. But then in dismay, I discovered the limits of literature, and launched into a long explanation to which he listened politely. René Maran was the first black writer to have received the Prix Goncourt in 1921 for his novel *Batouala*. But he had paid dearly for his reputation and his condemnation of the colonial regime. He had been stripped of his function as colonial administrator.

Sheepishly, Uncle Jean promised to read *Batouala*.

After coffee, while the others played cards and parlour games, Madame Sulpice drew me aside. Her face was solemn and her voice serious. Didn't I have a mother, aunts or older sisters to advise me? It was breaking her heart to see me undertake such a voyage and commit myself to Africa's formidable unknown, so young, alone and with an infant! Could she help me in some way? Did I need money? Once again I sensed the kindness of a stranger. And that is why I will not let anyone say that the world is composed of an apathetic bunch of egoists. I reassured Madame Sulpice as best I could.

At the end of the afternoon, Denis and I made our way back to the port accompanied by the entire Sulpice family, even Claire pushing Béatrice's wheelchair. We passed through a neighbourhood where the sounds of music—so strange and so harmonious—drifted out from behind the fence of a compound. I ventured in. A group of musicians was playing in front of an audience of women and children who willingly made room for us. I had never seen a griot before. I had never heard a *kora* or a *balafon*. I knew only of the poems Senghor had composed for these instruments. I stayed so long in that courtyard out of pure delight that I almost missed the ship.

I still remember the lights of the town slowly fading into the distance.

We set sail again into a rough sea. At dawn, we had to confront a terrible storm. The sky was streaked with lightning. Waves 7 metres high sent the *Mermoz* pitching left and right while torrents of water rained down upon the passengers shivering under tarpaulins on deck. I kept cool, and dabbed Denis's forehead with camphorated alcohol and felt, despite it all, that I was indestructible. The bad weather lasted two days before the sun came out. And it was a glorious morning the day we docked in Abidjan. A van from the college in Bingerville was waiting for me. To my great regret I saw nothing of the town, for the driver drove through it at breakneck speed. Bingerville had not yet become a virtual suburb of Abidjan. A thick forest of trees with elephant-like trunks separated the two conglomerations. The forest was bathed in darkness; here and there, the sun's rays broke through the leaf canopy. Thousands of birds and insects made a deafening noise. One of my novels (*Who Slashed*

*Celanire's Throat*?) is largely inspired by my first impressions of the Ivory Coast. Like my heroine, Célanire, I was shivering from an irrational feeling of anguish which at the same time I relished.

At Bingerville, I was in for an unpleasant surprise. At that time, in Africa, the French Antilleans, especially the Martinicans, were numerous in the teaching profession. Monsieur Blérald, the college principal, was a mulatto from Fort de France whose wife with the maiden name of Mademoiselle Gervaise had once been an auxiliary in Guadeloupe. She had therefore been my French teacher when I was a brilliant student at the Cours Michelet. She couldn't believe her eyes when she saw me again in such a modest establishment. She was convinced that I had been admitted to the Ecole Normale Supérieure and was sailing through the upper echelons of some prestigious French lycée.

Amazement and disappointment were written all over her face. 'I couldn't believe it was the same person!' she exclaimed. 'I was looking for the name Maryse Boucolon in the Ministry's correspondence. Whatever happened?'

I did not like her pitying tone of voice. And I explained in an offhand manner that I had been gripped by a violent desire to change the routine of my life. So I had ditched my studies and left for Africa. She was not entirely fooled by my assurance. Consequently, our relationship was always strained. She treated me like a young relative and would have liked me to confide in her. But I put her interest down to an unhealthy curiosity and was reluctant to confide in her. When she saw I was pregnant, she murmured by way of a reproach: 'Why didn't you tell me?'

Her pity revolted me.

The college boasted a music teacher, a Guadeloupean and the sister of Gabriel Lisette, one of the political celebrities of that time. A former colonial administrator, Lisette disproved Uncle Jean. In 1947, he had founded the Parti Progressiste Tchadien, a local section of Félix Houphouët-Boigny's Rassemblement Démocratique Africain (RDA). A loyal admirer of General de Gaulle, he supported the idea of a French Commonwealth and campaigned for a gradual and pacific decolonization of the African continent.

Mademoiselle Lisette had been a frequent visitor to my parents' home. She too treated me like a relative but never insisted on interrogating me. Despite our age difference, we became the best of friends. She suffered from a serious neurological illness, or perhaps the after-effects of a stroke, which affected her mobility and her elocution. For this reason, she was the laughing stock of her students who, every afternoon, followed her to her garden gate, shouting insults and jibes. I cannot judge the quality of her teaching. But I can testify to her intelligence, her

•

sensitivity and her gentleness. She invited me on long walks in the surrounding forest which she bravely explored, and talked to me about Africa in her halting, stuttering way. Unlike her brother, she was just as negative as Uncle Jean. She too sighed bitterly that the Africans loathed us Antilleans.

Her explanation, however, was different: 'They're jealous of us. They think we're too close to the French who trust us because they consider us superior to the Africans.'

I hadn't yet formed a valid opinion on this issue. So I didn't say a word. 'I keep warning Gabriel,' she continued, 'but he won't listen—he's so devoted to the Chadians. One day, they'll tell him face to face that he is not one of theirs.'

Unfortunately, she was clairvoyant. Gabriel Lisette was considered the mastermind behind the plots opposing the North of Chad with the South. Forced into exile, he had to abandon everything and return to Paris where Michel Debré offered him the job of minister counsellor to the government.

The little town of Bingerville had a certain charm about it. At one point, the capital of the Ivory Coast, it lay in the shadow of the Orphanage for Half-Castes, an enormous stone edifice dating from the colonial era (and featured in *Who Slashed Celanire's Throat?*) The institution took in the offspring of the

French colonials and the local Ivorian women. In most cases, the mother and the mother's family did not want the child any more than the father, already back in France. When I was living in Bingerville, the orphanage had taken in the last of the children. You could see them, pale-faced and disowned by their parents, dragging their feet along the streets, accompanied by monitors with the looks of martinets.

There was also a leper house, the source of much infuriation among the many Antillean and French members working at every echelon of the colonial administration. Because the patients could come and go as they pleased, exhibiting their horribly deformed faces and limbs. There were many posters on public display asserting that leprosy, despite its dramatic effects, was by no means contagious—but nobody believed them.

One or two kilometres from the small town there was a magnificent horticultural garden, a genuine paradise where rare plants, from every corner of the globe, grew.

I could have curled up and enjoyed a peaceful existence in Bingerville's reassuring cocoon: during the week, prepare my lessons, very basic given the level of the pupils; on weekends, have lunch or dinner with one or other of my compatriots followed by never-ending games of belote; during the holidays, visit the other Guadeloupeans and Martinicans posted to Bouaké, Man or other outlying regions.

I realized then that the French Antilleans lived solely among themselves. Throughout the African continent, a huge gap separated them from the Africans and I was tempted to elaborate an opinion on why that was so. I refused to believe, as was commonly the case, that the Africans loathed the Antilleans. That the latter thought themselves superior which the Africans felt they had no reason to do. Weren't they former slaves, the Africans would say in contempt, failing to distinguish between domestic slavery and the Atlantic slave trade. Since such an assertion seemed simplistic, I preferred to think that the Africans didn't understand the Antilleans' unwitting Westernization; that is what they found offensive.

As for the Antilleans, Africa was a mysterious and incomprehensible landscape which, in the end, frightened them. I, on the contrary, was attracted to and intrigued by it. I began with Jiman, my house boy, as a research topic. Going by his white mop of hair, he was old enough to be my father. One day, he stopped in front of a hedge I was trimming as best I could and offered his services for an amount I thought ridiculous. He came from the sands of Niger and opened my eyes to poverty, the painful need for exile and the search for survival. He was the one who told me of the violent inter-tribal conflicts and the pogroms of the previous year, in October 1958, against the Dahomeyans. Dahomey, once the Latin Quarter of

Africa because of its high level of education, was unable to feed its children who were attracted to the obvious prosperity of the Ivory Coast. In the years to come, all kinds of immigrants flowed into Abidjan before they were drowned in xenophobia. Jiman was devoted to Denis, which made me somewhat ashamed of being a mother too consumed by her own demons and too remote.

'Is Jiman my grandaddy?' Denis once asked me in all seriousness.

Soon I extended my field of research while being courted by Koffi N'Guessan, director of the horticultural garden. Nothing happened between us, except him squeezing my hands and staring at me with his bovine eyes. Squat and pot-bellied, he was also polygamous, wedded to three or four wives and the father of a dozen children. I can't recall why I was touched by his attentions. Jiman was furious every time Koffi sent me trays loaded with succulent Ivorian dishes which he, Jiman, couldn't rival on account of my modest food budget: banana *foutu*, yam *foutu*, palm-nut stew, spinach stew, *kedgenou* and *attièkè*. Interestingly enough, Koffi was a great admirer of Houphouët-Boigny and had an important job in the local section of the RDA. He used to take me in his jeep to political meetings, although we never ventured further than the coastal region. The grey, flat ocean suddenly boiled with spray at the line of rollers. Clusters of young boys jostled each other in the water, yelling and braving death. Once we drove as far as Grand Bassam. The atmosphere was melancholic, the ocean flat and heaving until it reached the line of waves. While Koffi dived into the party headquarters I wandered along the paved streets, imaging the time when ships owned by the rich merchant companies from Bordeaux and Nantes anchored beyond the line of rollers and waited for their cargo. Swimmers and fleets of canoes would bring in drums of palm oil. I walked into a former warehouse falling into ruin. Grand Bassam was dying. Tourism hadn't been able to revive it and the civil war and confrontations between Laurent Gbagbo and Alassane Wattara would destroy what remained.

I didn't understand very much at the political meetings I attended since the speakers spoke in their own language. For me they were performances, baroque and impenetrable operas, whose librettos were out of reach. I was impressed by the huge presence of women, dressed in elegantly patterned wrappers printed with the slogans 'Long live Houphouët-Boigny', 'Long live Philippe Yacé', 'Long live the RDA', by the fiery speeches, the patriotic songs and the frenzied tirades of the griots. In my first novel *Heremakhonon* (1976), although the action was inspired by the events in Guinea when the young hero Birame III, convinced that the ideals of the Revolution have been betrayed, refuses to surrender,

I attribute to his teacher, French Antillean Veronica, the same feelings these meetings aroused in me.

In the Ivory Coast, I felt that a new Africa was striving to be born, an Africa that would rely solely on its own resources, that would rid itself of the arrogance and paternalism of its colonizers.

I also got the painful feeling that I was being kept on the sidelines.

Shortly afterwards I went down to the port of Abidjan to greet Guy Tirolien who was returning to his post following an assignment in France.

I have already mentioned that Guy had divorced my sister Ena and as a result our two families, once so proud of the marriage (because the families of the Grands Nègres had married their children and created a dynasty), had been in an open feud. I remained on good terms with Guy because his second wife, Thérèse, had been at school with me in Pointe-à-Pitre. But that wasn't the only reason. Guy and I felt oddly close to one another. I admired his intelligence, his modesty, his determination; I considered him almost a model. He was one of those colonial administrators who belied Uncle Jean. A fervent adept of the RDA as well; in every post he had occupied since 1944, he had worked to bring Antilleans and Africans together with the prospect of emancipating them. In Paris, he was, together with Alioune Diop, one of the founders of *Présence Africaine*.

•

We threw our arms around each other.

'How do you like Africa?' he thundered.

I stammered that I did like it. But I had only just arrived in the Ivory Coast and knew very little about it.

'You must love it!' he asserted. 'She's mother to us all and has suffered so much.'

Thereupon he launched into a panegyric on Houphouët-Boigny, soon to be elected president. He had abolished porterage and hard labour. He was working for the emancipation of the black man. Listening to him, I couldn't help gazing at Thérèse's mother who was accompanying them to take care of their three young children. How I would have liked my mother to be with me, although Jeanne Quidal would have been too proud to follow me into this godforsaken hole of Africa.

Thérèse could see I was sad. 'How are you?' she whispered in quite a different tone of voice. 'Not too tired?'

I assured her I wasn't. We had lunch together and then I took a taxi back to the bus station. That visit left me with a bitter taste in my heart. I felt so alone in Bingerville, ill-equipped to help the Africa who needed it so much.

From that moment on, I never refused an outing with Koffi N'Guessan. As soon as I finished teaching, I jumped into a bush taxi to visit Abidjan. My eye registered everything like a camera: the corpulent mothers with their babies on their backs, seated on tiny little wooden stools and selling all kinds of food, the street hawkers and the policemen patrolling two by two. Although it hadn't yet achieved its status as the economic capital of West Africa (now set back by recent events), Abidjan was lively, even opulent. At that time, there was only one bridge over the lagoon, the Houphouët-Boigny Bridge built between 1954 and 1957. It was packed with cars, a good number driven by locals, hinting at a burgeoning middle class. The many suburbs surrounding the French quarter, Treichville, Adjamé and Marcory, were a pleasant and prosperous hive of activity. Far from the memories I had of Dakar!

But since I never spoke to anyone during these frequent excursions into town, I felt I wasn't making much progress in getting to know Africa. I was merely a spectator wherever I went. What I hadn't anticipated was that my past would catch up with me. Jocelyne Etienne, a Guadeloupean girl who had lived with me at the Pierre de Coubertin Hostel on the rue Lhomond, now had an important position at the Ministry of Culture. Nicole Sala, another Guadeloupean whom I had known in Paris, now lived in Abidjan. (Nicole had married an African— but that had by no means shocked our narrow little circle since Seiny Loum wasn't just anybody. A talented lawyer, he had been appointed one of Senegal's first ambassadors after independence.)

Jocelyne and Nicole, who entertained politicians and dignitaries, both African and Antillean, often invited me to their homes. Despite their cordial welcomes, I had the impression that they were acting out of solidarity towards their compatriot and in memory of our former ties. I thought I detected a certain embarrassment. I did look a sorry sight in the midst of that select assembly. An obscure teacher in a college way out in the bush, soon to be mother to a second infant with an absent father, I didn't even own a car, and travelled by bush taxi packed with Africans. I could have refused those invitations. But I never managed to. This divorce between intention and reality therefore was an excuse for some painful introspection. What was the basis for this hatred of the bourgeoisie I had begun to show? Wasn't my behaviour governed by the fact that I had excluded myself from 'polite society'? I had kept none of the promises I had tacitly made to my family and my milieu. As I recount in *Victoire, My Mother's Mother*, my father and mother both prided themselves on being Grands Nègres. By that they meant they had a mission to serve as an example for their entire Race. (We should note that the word 'Race' was not an issue as it is today). What would my parents think of their youngest daughter, the one with so much promise?

At the end of a lucid and cruel examination of my conscience, I arrived at the conclusion that I was a hypocrite.

•

It was then that I received a letter from Gillette informing me of the death of our father. As I have mentioned, my father had never liked me very much. Twice married, he had ten children: I was the last and, what's more, a girl. And, despite my conceited looks, he detected a weakness and a vulnerability which he disliked. And yet his death was a terrible blow to me. The island where I was born was nothing more than a graveyard. It was barred to me for ever. This second death unravelled the last knot which tied me to Guadeloupe. I was not only an orphan, I was also stateless, homeless, without a place of origin or belonging. At the same time, I felt a sense of liberation that was somewhat enjoyable, the feeling of now being free of any kind of judgement.

I was living in a state of mental malaise, seldom at peace with myself and often miserable, when I was overwhelmed by an extraordinarily happy event. On 3 April 1960, my first daughter, Sylvie-Anne, was born. My pregnancy had gone off without a hitch. No nausea, no cramps. I had been out walking with Denis and Mademoiselle Lisette when I discovered it was time to jump into the car of a Martinican colleague, Caristan, and set off for the central hospital in Abidjan. As soon as the midwife placed Sylvie-Anne in my arms, I was flooded with maternal love. As God is my witness, despite the conditions of his birth, I had never treated Denis as a whipping boy or a scapegoat. Yet, as he grew older, everything in him reminded me of his father, a man I now hated—the same light skin, the same smile, the same brown eyes, the same laugh and the same voice. The love I showered on him was always mixed with painful memories. Even recently, while watching a projection of *The Agronomist*, I don't know whether I was crying for my son or for Jean Dominique slaughtered like a dog. With Sylvie-Anne, everything was different. Everything was simple. Never had such a flow of tenderness flooded my heart. I would wake up at night, my heart beating, and dash over to her cradle to make sure my precious baby was alive. I would gaze at her for hours, in wonder.

It was with this power of love in mind that I wrote to Condé, something I had never done until then, and suggested he get to know his daughter. I felt that I didn't have the right to deprive this child of her father. Condé promptly replied that it would make him very happy, and invited me to come and join him in Guinea during the next long holiday.

On 7 August 1960, on the occasion of the independence celebrations in Abidjan, I squeezed into Koffi N'Guessan's jeep beside his two youngest wives (the two older ones had their own car). They were dressed identically in sumptuous, embroidered boubous, adorned with heavy jewellery and enormous head ties. They stared at me, curious and uneasy, as if I

•

were a strange animal of whom they did not know what to expect. I was a woman. They were women. Yet this did not bring us any closer.

'They don't speak French!' Koffi blurted out by way of introduction.

Since the outskirts of the city were cordoned off by lines of police, we had to park the jeep and continue on foot. The streets were packed. We had difficulty getting through, deafened by the beat of the drums and the shouts of the griots, avoiding as best we could the clowns, the acrobats and the dancers, some of whom were doing comical entrechats on their stilts. The two wives went into the offices of the RDA while Koffi and I stayed outside, under a hot sun, for an hour amid the tumult. Finally, Houphouët-Boigny appeared, in a car with the roof down and crawling along at a snail's pace. In a time when very few could afford a television, I had seen him only in the newspaper. I couldn't take my eyes off him. He was small, slightly built, his face a troubling and impenetrable mask as if carved in old leather. Waving his arms awkwardly, he repeated: 'All together, Whites and Blacks! Come on over to the edge of the road.'

The crowd screamed in jubilation. And I told myself I was witnessing an historic moment.

However much Koffi tried to explain that I had come all the way from Guadeloupe to attend the ceremony, the guards would not let me into the National Assembly where the inauguration was to take place. I had neither a personal invitation nor an RDA membership card nor a valid voter's card. I had to turn back, racked by a painful feeling of exclusion. This was the first time, but by no means the last, that I would feel that way in Africa.

At the bus station, I climbed into an empty bush taxi. The driver, with a mop of hair like a fetish child, gave me my first lesson in what is commonly called 'tribalism'. He seemed sullen and did not share at all the jubilation I had just witnessed.

'Why?' I asked him. 'Wasn't this a great day?'

'That Houphouët-Boigny there,' he replied, 'is a Baoulé. I'm a Bété.'

'What do you mean?'

He shrugged. 'What I mean is that now the Baoulé will have everything and me, a Bété, I'll go on getting nothing.'

Back in Bingerville I went to fetch Denis and Sylvie whom I had left with Caristan. Oblivious to the political events, they were playing a game of belote.

'Did it go all right?' Caristan asked me. Then, without waiting for my answer, he continued: 'It won't change a thing! The Whites will continue to lay down the law. Like Senghor, this Houphouët-Boigny is their creature. I don't know how many times he's been a minister in the French government. He's a pawn.'

•

Once again I couldn't voice an opinion. Caristan's viewpoint was the opposite of Guy and Koffi; for the latter, especially, Houphouët-Boigny was a leader as strong as an elephant, emblem of the RDA, solely concerned with emancipating his people.

I kept silent and accepted a cup of coffee from Madame Caristan.

A few days later Koffi plucked up courage and declared his undying love for me. He brandished in front of me the prospect of a job at the lycée in Abidjan, and showed me a flat where I would be housed during the next school year. The ultramodern flat with a view over the lagoon was magnificent. I had no use whatsoever for Koffi's feelings for me, but I couldn't see myself spending a second year in Bingerville. So I let myself be kissed and accepted his proposition. Nevertheless, the following week, I paid my beloved houseboy, Jiman, two months' salary and flew to Guinea with my two children as I had promised Condé.

If I endeavour to assess what I had gained from this first stay in Africa, I would be obliged to admit that the result was fairly meagre. During a visit to Bouaké, I acquired a collection of wooden Baoulé fertility dolls with strange round heads and rigid outstretched arms. Today they still stare at me with their empty eyes and seem symbolic to me. For I too saw nothing. I too heard nothing.

•

And yet the Ivory Coast, the first African country I landed in, left me with a series of indelible images. I shall never forget the wonder I felt as I entered the baroque cathedral of the forest on the way to Bingerville; how I was captivated by the remains of the colonial past at Grand Bassam; how I admired the beauty of the women, their hairstyles, the way they dressed and adorned themselves with jewels. As recently as 2010, when I was writing *En attendant la montée des eaux*, I couldn't help having Babakar, one of my heroes, live in Abidjan, even though the city had been ravaged by years of civil war. It was my way of expressing my sorrow and regret for what it had become.

I who later on was to make so many trips by plane—that was the first time I had flown. Like Denis, I was scared to death. With my nose pressed against the window I shivered at the sight of the thick dark green canopy of the forest below the plane, the blood red of the soil, the immensity and dazzle of the ocean.

*A Second Flight over a Second Cuckoo's Nest*

In 1960, Conakry couldn't stand comparison with Abidjan, not even with Bingerville. It was a conglomeration of no importance and its only adornment was the sea—purple, grandiose, breaking over jagged rocks. A few buildings had an acquired elegance about them: the administrative edifices, banks and state-owned shops. The rest were shapeless concrete constructions. The women crowded around the outdoor taps dripping water. The children they carried on their backs or dragged behind them all had the symptoms of kwashiorkor. Like the men, they wore threadbare clothes, almost rags. I had never lived in a country that was predominantly Muslim. I knew nothing about Islam. I was therefore distressed by the little *talibé* boys shivering in the cool of the dawn as they chanted Almighty God together with the beggars and the cripples crowding around the mosques. Lost in admiration I gazed at the elders sitting enthroned in the dust, their eyes glazed in meditation, rolling their beads. I admired the little boys dashing to the Koranic schools with their small boards under their arms. In short, I fell in love with a place that was totally destitute.

Of all the towns I have lived in, Conakry remains dearest to my heart. It was my real port of entry into Africa. It made me understand 'under-development'. I witnessed the arrogance of the privileged and the destitution of the weak.

The day I arrived at the airport, Condé embraced with equal tenderness his daughter Sylvie and Denis whom he was seeing for the first time.

'Can I call you Papa?' Denis asked.

'But I am your Papa!' Condé answered with a burst of laughter.


As incredible as it may seem, this was the only allu-sion we made to Denis's situation. We never spoke of Jean Dominique. Condé never sought to know who Denis's father was nor the circumstances of his birth. No doubt Condé saw things all too clearly despite his silence. He knew that Africa was largely a refuge for me. He knew that if it hadn't been for my painful past, I would never have married him. This was the most unnerving of the things left unsaid. I have to admit that in his undemonstrative way he adopted Denis and never treated him any differently from the children we had later.

Condé was accompanied by Sékou Kaba, a former school friend who was now private secretary to the minister of public service. This slender, taciturn man was to become my unfailing support. I, who had always kept in my thoughts my older brother, Guy, Guito, carried off at the age of twenty by our family illness that gradually destroyed one's balance, elocution and mobility, and that took the other members of my family, one by one, I found in Sékou Kaba a big brother and a mentor. There was never anything passionate or sexual between us. Member of a labour union, he had shared a room with Sékou Touré while studying in Dakar. He no longer saw him now that he was president, but worshipped him like a god. He taught me 'African socialism' and had me read the indigestible volumes published locally on the history and role of the Parti Démocratique de Guinée (PDG) as well as hagiographies of the president and some of his ministers.

Since Condé and I did not have much money, we lodged at his place. His modest villa was situated in the densely populated district of the port and, besides his wife and two daughters, it housed a multitude of brothers, sisters, cousins, brothers-in-law and sisters-in-law. Located next to a mosque, we were woken up every morning by the first call to prayer which I never got used to and which never failed to force me out of bed and onto my knees. Listening to the muezzin's insistent voice, I dreamt of achieving some great deed.

•

But what?

Condé looked at me from the bed: 'Too excited, my dear! You're too excited!' he scoffed.

However hard I tried, I never managed to make close contact with Gnalengbè, Sékou's wife, whereas I would have so liked her to treat me like an older sister. I could hear her laughing and chatting in the kitchen. But as soon as I appeared she would go silent and withdraw.

I ended up complaining to Sékou: 'Do I frighten her?'

'You intimidate her!' he replied after a slight hesitation. 'She can't speak French. She hardly went to school. She wears traditional wraps, you understand? She has a slight complex. If you learnt Malinké, you might get to know her better.'

This frequently repeated suggestion began to exasperate me because I quickly realized that if I wanted to decode African societies, I would have to converse with the people. But which language should I choose out of so many?

'Learn Malinké!' said a Malinké.

'Learn Fulani!' said a Peul.

'Learn Soussou!' said a Soussou.

Sékou could not resign himself to my situation with Condé and would not hear of a divorce. He begged me to abandon the Ivory Coast for Guinea where, given his high position, he was confident of finding me a teaching job. It was due to his affectionate insistence that one morning I found myself heading to the Immigration Services. Waving my brand-new family registration book, I demanded a Guinean passport. There was no ambiguity about it: it was neither a political decision nor a militant act of faith. There was no doubt I was happy to surrender my French nationality. But for me, above all, it was a demonstration of freedom. This material reappropriation of Africa proved to me that by going one step further than the leader of the Negritude movement, my intellectual guide, I had begun to come to terms with myself.

'Fill these out!' barked an employee, setting on the counter a small pile of forms.

'There's no need for that!' asserted another agent emerging from behind him. Sweeping up the pile of documents, he explained conceitedly: 'Guinean nationality is given in addition to the one she has because of her marriage. It's a plus and an asset.'

I confess I didn't understand a word he was saying. But no matter—I gaily pocketed the magnificent green document I had been issued, little knowing that later it would burn my fingers. I could not imagine that there would come a day when I would recuperate my French nationality and thank heaven that I had not filled out any form, rightly or wrongly, at that time.

As for Condé: he pretended not to intervene in my decisions and never proposed we get together again. I wonder if he hadn't guessed that, sooner or later, we would separate. He took care of the children like a father. He would bathe Sylvie-Anne and rub her body with a bundle of dried herbs. And every afternoon he would slip on a pair of shorts and a T-shirt and call out to Denis: 'Come on! Let's play ball.'

And Denis would follow him, beside himself with happiness.

*History Repeats Itself . . .*
*Without Saying the Same Thing Twice*

I stayed only a few weeks in Guinea, then flew to France with Denis and Sylvie. The Guinean air fleet comprised very comfortable, brand-new Russian Ilyushin 18 planes. I still wonder why I came back to Paris and why I didn't spend the remainder of my holiday in Conakry. For me, the French capital remained full of painful memories. Ena continued to ignore me, and Gillette said she was too busy to see me too often. As for my only friends: Eddie was finishing her studies in Rheims whereas Yvane was even further away. Just married to a French agronomist, she was living in Dschang, Cameroon. Perhaps it was because I wanted to be like the colonial civil servants whose holidays in France were sacred. I also think that since nobody, nowhere, was waiting for me, I whiled away my solitude as best I could.

And then: Why would I stay on at Sékou Kaba's? Life there was devoid of any charm. While Condé,

.

who took the gift of *farniente* to the extreme, slept all morning long, I bored myself to death reading the indigestible volumes of the history of the PDG. When Sékou came home from work, we dined in a hubbub of children crying, quarrels between wives and co-wives, griots yelling on the radio and the cheering from a stadium close by. I had the choice then of either staying to listen to incomprehensible programs in the national language while Gnalengbè and her buddies guffawed in the kitchen or spend the evening out with Condé and Sékou. I soon realized this was the wrong choice. Their friends would sit me down with a glass of tamarind juice and then totally forget about me while they embarked on yet another noisy and never-ending conversation in Malinké. I ended up staying home, lying on my bed and reading the history of the PDG while Gnalengbè and her buddies had the time of their lives in the sitting room.

Gradually, I came to understand it was not enough to learn Malinké—I also needed to understand that the world was composed of two distinct hemispheres, that of men and that of women.

I wasn't enthusiastic about being back in Paris. With the little money I had, I entrusted Sylvie and Denis to Madame Bonenfant who almost fainted with joy. This time, I paid her in advance. Then I booked a room at the Cité Universitaire on the Boulevard

Jourdan. And I spent my time as best I could. Mornings, I would stroll through the streets, poking into bookstores and visiting museums and art galleries. Afternoons, I spent satisfying my passion for the cinema. At the Luxembourg I attended a retrospective of Louis Malle, and watched films such as *Elevator for the Gallows*, *The Lovers* and *Zazie in the Metro* for the first time.

I also mastered the art of rebuffing the lovers of exoticism who harassed me.

It was then that I experienced what I call my second Haitian passion. It was so different from the first that you might think fate was either offering me revenge or, frankly, making a mockery. Playing a trick on me in its unique way. Bringing the Haiti that had destroyed me back into my life.

One evening, as I was returning from the university cafeteria, a group of young students approached me.

'Are you Haitian, mademoiselle?'

They were about half a dozen. One in particular caught my attention. His name was Jacques V . . . He was not very tall. Since I am tall myself, I've always had a weakness for small men. Shiny black skin, thick sensual lips, a large forehead crowned with a mass of curly hair and a melancholic look in his eyes. I was also struck by the respect he commanded from his colleagues, as he was the illegitimate son of François Duvalier, president of Haiti, despite Jean Dominique's efforts. Duvalier had soon turned out to be a ruthless dictator, a 'Tropical Moloch', according to the expression by filmmaker Raoul Peck. Under his command, the Tontons Macoutes laid down the law, massacring whole families while others headed straight for exile. This horrible political reality, however, never came between us. We never talked of culture or literature. The world vanished around us. The sounds of the outside world never managed to pierce the fabulous void in which we had shrouded ourselves. In June 1960, the Belgian Congo had achieved independence. In July, the province of Katanga seceded. Lumumba, Kasa-Vubu, Tschombé, Mobutu—these names that emerged out of the equatorial forest made headlines on the pages of the newspapers we never read.

All that mattered was the uncontrollable desire we felt for each other.

This time it was not a noble intellectual kind of love—it was a voracious dialogue of bodies. For weeks we remained locked in his room, without speaking a word, without eating a morsel except for the occasional slice of bread with a bit of peanut butter. Making love. Emerging only at night to visit the Elysée Matignon or La Cabane Cubaine nightclubs. If I say Jacques loved dancing, it would be an understatement—he danced with the same ardour and passion and fury as when he made love. It was the golden age of the Afro-Cubans—mambos, cha-cha-chas. Celia Cruz, Sonora Matancera and the Orquestra Aragon were kings.

I had never known how to dance. I had been brought up by my parents to mock and despise those attributes which the West endows on black folks, including the sense of rhythm and heightened sensuality. Although now I understand that Jacques used his body to demonstrate a freedom that I had been cruelly deprived of, I did not attempt to imitate him while he whirled around the dance floor amid the applause of the other dancers. I knew I would look ridiculous. Petrified with envy, I stayed at my table, huddled over a glass of planter's punch and tried to put on a good face.

We remained out clubbing until the early hours of the morning. When we emerged, Paris was grey-hued and the Sarakollé street cleaners dressed in fluorescent overalls were capering through its streets. We would dive into the first metro, full of sleepy revellers, and lock ourselves up again in the Cité Universitaire. I won't let anyone blame me for having made love to the son of one of the most bloodthirsty dictators the world has known. Jacques was not like that for me. I was living a passion. Passion defies analysis and does not moralize. It burns, blazes and consumes.

And yet, half-way through October, I plucked up enough courage to return to my room without waking Jacques who was exhausted and snoring. I feverishly packed my cases and in a fog took the first train to Chartres. There I collected Sylvie and Denis and flew back to Guinea from Orly. I have never really understood why I inflicted such a wound on myself. I believe now that it was the result of a warped maternal feeling—I was convinced I was acting for the good of my children. Enough of this rashness! Enough of this egotism! Denis and Sylvie-Anne were not meant to grow up in the anomaly of a one-parent household. They had to have a country, a home and a father. Their country was Guinea, their home was Conakry and their father was Condé. I still wonder how I managed to get back to Conakry. Shortly after I arrived, I fainted in Sékou Kaba's car. He was terrified. Soon I became so weak that I had to take to my bed. I had constant dizzy fits and fainting spells. Incapable even of drinking, eating, washing and dressing, I spent most of my time prostrate in my bedroom.

'Maman, you're not going to die, are you?' Denis whispered.

I hugged him without being able to say a word.

Gnalengbè and Condé put my condition down to malaria, then rampant in the country, a real epidemic. Gnalengbè made me swallow tablets of quinine and cups of quinquéliba, a bitter herb tea apparently able to cure everything.

Condé did not attempt to ask me what might have happened during my stay in Paris for I was visibly in a state of shock, moving like a zombie and jumping when anyone addressed me. Without a word of protest, Condé unrolled a sleeping mat in the living room amid a group of astonished teenage relatives when I plucked up enough courage to tell him that I could no longer stand being in contact with him. Sékou Kaba was filled with dismay as he witnessed the debacle of our relationship.

In the meantime, a letter from Eddie informed me that Jacques had travelled as far as Rheims to ask her for my address in Conakry. His behaviour and his intentions were those of a mad man; he talked of coming to Guinea to get me at the head of a squadron of Tontons Macoutes who would simply kill Condé since they were used to such crimes. And he would then take me back to Haiti.

Since my health worsened, I ended up consulting a Polish doctor in a neighbouring dispensary. He informed me that I was pregnant again.

Pregnant!

I cried my heart out—a child was the last thing I wanted. I obviously didn't believe a word of Koffi's hasty promise to set me up in Abidjan. Nevertheless, once again, I felt I was the victim of fate.

This pregnancy tied me inexorably to Condé and to Guinea.

I had no other way out.

*'We Prefer Being Poor and Free
to Being Rich and Enslaved'*

Sékou Touré

Everything moved very quickly. Thanks to Sékou Kaba, who was very happy at how my condition was improving, I was appointed French teacher at the girls' college in Bellevue, situated in a pretty colonial building nestling in a tangle of greenery on the outskirts of Conakry. The principal was a charming Martinican woman called Madame Batchily, since Antilleans could be found at every level of the educational system both in Guinea and the Ivory Coast. Those, however, who were in a rush to work in Guinea had nothing in common with those working in the Ivory Coast. They were not interested in forming an affable community, preoccupied with making black sausage and cod fritters. Highly politicized, Marxists of course, they had crossed the Atlantic to offer their skills to the young nation which sorely needed them. When they got together at each other's houses over a glass of quinquéliba (this tea really had so many virtues!) they discussed the thoughts of Gramsci, Marx or Hegel. I can't remember why I decided to attend one of those. It was held in a villa belonging to a Guadeloupean by the name of MacFarlane, a philosophy teacher, married to a pretty French woman.

'I hear you're a Boucolon,' he whispered politely to my surprise. 'I grew up next to your home on the rue Dugommier. I was a close friend of Auguste.'

Auguste was my older brother, twenty-five years older, with whom I had never been very close. He was the pride of the family, being the first to hold an *aggregation* in classics in Guadeloupe. Unfortunately, he never claimed to have any political ambition and lived all his life, totally incognito, in a suburban house in Asnières. Understandably, any comparison with him terrified me. It seemed that whatever I did, I was to be tracked down. If I wasn't careful, the Grands Nègres might very well catch up with me.

'Is your husband in Paris?' he continued.

I mumbled that he was finishing his studies.

'What was he studying?'

'He wants to be an actor and is studying at the Conservatory on the rue Blanche.'

By his expression I could see he didn't think much of such a vocation. He moved away and then inflicted on us, for over an hour, his reading of some obscure political essay by an equally obscure writer.

•

From that moment on, I carefully avoided that circle of left-wing pedants and decided to break ties with my own community. But I did not fully keep my word and made one exception. One of Madame Batchily's two sisters, who had followed on her heels to Guinea, was an *agrégée* in history and taught at the lycée in Donka. Her name was Yolande. She was lovely and sophisticated, and president of the association of history teachers in Guinea. Despite her titles, we became very close. Like several other compatriots, we were housed in the Residence Boulbinet, two ten-storey towers, oddly modern, in an unlikely spot facing the sea, in a modest fisherman's neighbourhood. Since the lift never worked, Yolande would stop at my place on the first floor before beginning the climb up to her flat on the tenth. She lived with Louis, a Benin prince, a direct descendant of King Gbéhanzin, an opponent of French colonialism, who was exiled to Fort-de-France in Martinique and who then died in Blida, Algeria. Louis owned a collection of artefacts which once belonged to his ancestor: a pipe, a snuff box and a pair of nail scissors. Above all, he possessed numerous photos of the old king. That face, both intelligent and determined, gave me much food for thought. To my surprise, it came back to me years later and encouraged me to write my novel *The Last of the African Kings*. I imagined his exile in Martinique and people mocking him: 'An African king? What on earth is that?'

More than anything, I imagined him being terrified by our violent storms and the fury of our hurricanes, elements he was not used to. I gave him an Antillean descendant in the person of Spero and liked to think he kept a diary.

Louis Gbéhanzin was an extremely intelligent man and history teacher at the Donka lycée. He had Sékou Touré's ear, and was the architect behind the educational reform, a colossal enterprise which was never completed. Although the idea of confiding in Yolande never occurred to me, I felt a deep admiration for her and a genuine friendship. Her outspokenness did me good for she often scolded me in no uncertain terms: 'How live such a vegetable-like existence when you're so intelligent?'

Was I still intelligent?

Nobody could guess how unhappy I was, to the point of often wishing that I was dead. Yolande and Louis attributed my moroseness and apathy to the absence of Condé who had returned to Paris for his final year at the conservatory. He had accepted the news of my pregnancy with stoicism.

'This time it will be a boy!' he had claimed as if that would sweeten the pill. 'And we'll call him Alexander.'

'Alexander!' I cried, recalling the fuss my choice of the Westernized name of Sylvie-Anne had caused. 'But it's not Malinké.'

•

'No matter!' he retorted. 'It's the name of a conqueror and my son will be a conqueror.'

We were never to have a son together whereas he had two or three with a second wife.

When Eddie wrote to say that Condé was having an affair with a Martinican actress, I must admit I couldn't have cared less. All I could think of was Jacques, and hating myself over and over again for how absurdly I had behaved. Why had I left him?

It was beyond understanding.

The day before term began at the Bellevue college, Madame Batchily assembled all the teachers in the staff room. They were all 'expats', a large contingent of French communists, political refugees from sub-Saharan Africa or the Maghreb and two Malagasies. Over a goblet of ersatz coffee, and nibbling on very dry cakes, she explained that our pupils came from families where the girls had never received a secondary education. At best, a mother had attended one or two years at elementary school and knew just about how to sign her name. So they felt ill at ease at a school desk and would prefer to be in the kitchen or at the market selling trinkets. We should therefore take extra care at getting them interested in our lessons.

Given my state of mind, such a discourse had no effect on me. Whereas in the years to come I was to devote so much of my attention to young people, I then took no interest whatsoever in my students

•

whom I considered lifeless and stupid. Very quickly my lessons became boring and a chore, reduced to exercises in elocution, spelling and grammar. At best, I analysed excerpts from books chosen by the mysterious Committees for Education and Culture who, as part of the reform, decided everything. In French, their selection was based on books with a sociological content rather than literary merit. It was therefore somewhat of a surprise that 'The Prayer of a Little Black Child' by Guadeloupean poet Guy Tirolien appeared in all the 'revised' textbooks.

When I was not at school and tried to read, the characters danced over the page. I no longer listened to the radio, unable to bear the never-ending vociferations of the griots. I was slowly coming to loathe the country. All I looked forward to were the nights when my dreams brought Jacques back to me.

Only Denis and Sylvie kept me alive. They were adorable. They showered my face with kisses. But I had become so sad, so taciturn (it was then that I forgot how to smile) that their caresses made me feel gloomier.

From the balcony of my apartment I witnessed every afternoon an amazing spectacle. At five thirty, President Sékou Touré, bare-headed, stunningly handsome in his ample white boubou, drove himself along the seafront in his Mercedes 280 SL convertible. He was cheered by the fishermen, who would leave their nets on the sand to crowd along the edge of the road. Apparently I was the only one upset by

•

the contrast between this all-powerful man and the miserable wretches in rags who applauded him.

'What a wonderful example of democracy!' Yolande and Louis reiterated.

'And no bodyguards!' added Sékou Kaba.

Guinea was the only French-speaking country in Africa to boast of having achieved a socialist revolution. The privileged no longer drove French cars but Skodas and Volgas. The lucky ones who left on holiday flew off in Ilyushin 18s or Tupolevs. Each district had its state-owned store where we were forced to shop, since all private commerce had been abolished. These stores were always poorly stocked and so bartering was the only arm we had against rationing and constant shortages. Precious foodstuffs were exchanged clandestinely because bartering was forbidden, supposedly to discourage the black market. There were inspectors and controllers everywhere whom everybody feared. I learnt to avoid concentrated milk from Czechoslovakia for it gave the children deadly diarrhoea (one almost killed Sylvie-Anne) and to distrust Russian sugar for it never melted, even in boiling liquids. Cheese, flour and cooking oil couldn't be found anywhere. I have often recounted how I came to find the title of my first novel *Heremakhonon*, largely inspired by my stay in Guinea and a Malinké expression meaning 'wait for happiness'. It was the name of the state-owned store in the Boulbinet district. It was always empty. And all the answers by the shop girls began with 'tomorrow', like an unfulfilled hope:

'Tomorrow there'll be cooking oil!'

'Tomorrow there'll be tomatoes!'

'Tomorrow there'll be sardines!'

'Tomorrow there'll be rice!'

Two events that occurred early in 1961 come to mind, events so different they prove that the heart does not prioritize—it puts the universal and the specific on the same level. On 4 January, Jiman, whom I had sent for from the Ivory Coast with the help of Sékou Kaba, returned home after several months in Guinea, fed up with the shortages that affected his work as a cook.

'A country that doesn't even have cooking oil!' he would repeat, outraged. He probably hadn't meditated long enough on Sékou Touré's famous phrase that beautifully stated: 'We prefer being poor and free to being rich and enslaved.' Whatever the case, even though he could be termed a vile counter-revolutionary, as the expression goes, I cried a river of tears standing on the wharf below the ship that was to take him back to his country's golden subjection, holding back a plea not to abandon me as well.

On the 17th of the same month, Patrice Lumumba was assassinated in the Congo. Guinea decreed four days of national mourning. I would like to write that I was very upset by the event. But I wasn't. I have already said that I took little interest in the initial convulsions of the ex-Belgian Congo. The name Lumumba meant nothing to me.

I did, nevertheless, go to Martyrs Square where a ceremonial homage was to be paid to Lumumba. I slipped into a dense crowd kept at a distance from the official platform by barriers and armed men. It was like attending a fashion show. The ministers, deputy ministers and dignitaries were accompanied by wives draped in luxurious traditional wrappers. Some wore voluminous head ties. Others displayed complicated hairstyles woven into rosettes or triangles. The impression of a show was reinforced by the applause and cheers from the crowd every time a couple of notables got out of their car and headed for the platform. Under a ceremonial canopy, Sékou Touré, dressed in his handsome white boubou, gave a speech that lasted for hours. He drew a lesson from the Congolese tragedy, emphasizing the words Capitalism and Oppression. And yet I don't know why his words sounded hollow.

I wondered where this Guinean revolution he was speaking of had gone.

I had to wait for the mediation of literature and the publication of Césaire's *A Season in the Congo* in 1965 to be really moved by this drama and realize its implication.

I was still not adequately politicized, no doubt.

I could have borne the deprivations that cast a pall over our lives if they had involved the entire population in a collective effort to build a free nation. It could even have been elating. But it was obviously not the case. Every day the nation was divided more and more into two groups separated by an impassable ocean of prejudice. Whereas we jolted along in crowded, ramshackle buses, brand-new Mercedes with pennants flying would overtake us, chauffeuring women dressed in their finest and covered in jewels and the men ostentatiously smoking Havana cigars ringed with their initials. Whereas we lined up outside the state-owned stores for a few kilos of rice, the privileged few treated themselves to caviar, foie gras and fine wines in shops where everything was paid for in foreign currency.

One day, Sékou Kaba proudly announced he had obtained tickets to a private concert at the president's palace. It was the first time I was about to enter the world of the privileged. I borrowed a boubou from Gnalengbè to hide my belly and clasped around my neck my Creole necklace. Thus dressed up I went to listen to the Republic's Traditional Music Ensemble. The main attraction of the evening was Sory Kandia Kouyaté, nicknamed 'The Mandé Star', who fully deserved such a hyperbole—no voice could compare to his. He was accompanied by other griots and over thirty musicians playing the kora, the balafon, the African guitar and the underarm drum. I have never seen such a show—it was dazzling, unforgettable and

incomparable. During the interval, when the spectators dashed to the bar, I was deeply shocked to
see Muslims in traditional dress gorging on pink
champagne and smoking Havana cigars. Discreetly,
Sékou Kaba led me to a group and introduced me to
the president, his brother Ismaël, the regime's right-
hand man, and a few ministers. The latter paid no
attention to me whatsoever. Only the president
feigned interest. Sékou Touré was even more handsome close up, with his oblique eyes and the winning
smile of a womanizer. Once Sékou Kaba had made
the introductions, he murmured: 'So you are from
Guadeloupe. You're one of the little sisters that
Africa once lost and now found again.'

I reported this conversation in *Heremakhonon*
when the dictator Malimwana enters Veronica's
classroom and converses with her. But I didn't possess Veronica's nerve who dared to replace the word
'lost' by 'sold'. So I was merely content to smile
obligingly. Sékou Touré moved off towards other
guests. The adulation he inspired was palpable.
People kissed his hands. Others went down on their
knees in front of him and he helped them up good-
naturedly. In the background, you could hear the
recitation of the griots, swelling now and then like
the chorus in an opera.

A bell announced that the interval was over, and
we went back to our seats.

## 'In Pain Thou Shalt Bring Forth Children'

*Genesis*

I dragged an enormous belly around the college and frightened my students, as Oumou Awa confessed when we met up again in 1992 at the Center for African Studies at Cornell: 'First of all: you intimidated us. Then: you took no interest in us. We thought your pregnancy both terrifying and mysterious.'

More prosaically, I could hardly walk—my legs were so painful and my feet so swollen that I had difficulty putting on my shoes. Since maternity leave had been abolished in socialist Guinea, women worked right up to their due date and then enjoyed a generous one month's rest for breastfeeding. In May 1961, I released a bucket of dirty water onto the floor of my classroom. Panic-stricken, Madame Batchily herself drove me in her Skoda to the Donka hospital.

'Your husband isn't here!' she said, visibly upset. 'Who do you want me to notify?'

•

I murmured the names of Sékou Kaba and Gnalengbè. I was very downhearted. Although my pregnancy in Abidjan had gone off without a hitch, I dreaded this one. The French physicians who had left in 1958 had been replaced by doctors from Eastern Europe, Russians, Poles, Czechs and Germans, who communicated with their patients via an interpreter. The hospital lacked everything. Shredded linen replaced cotton swabs; surgical spirit and ether were rationed. There were virtually no painkillers. The children died from measles, malaria and whooping cough; grown-ups from diarrhoea and all kinds of infections not yet known as nosoco-mial infection. A nauseating smell permeated the dilapidated buildings dating back to colonial times. The memory of what I endured there still remains with me and wakes me up at night.

On my arrival in the maternity ward, a Czech doctor in a coat of questionable cleanliness, accompanied by two Russian nurses, equally filthy, roughly examined me. Then one of the nurses motioned to me to follow her into a ward where a dozen pregnant women were writhing in pain, stretched out on dirty benches. I made room for myself and did the same. Very soon, however, I was the only one to combine contortions with screams. Nobody around me was lamenting. My wild, stressful screams echoed in a general silence.

'Aren't you ashamed of yourself, little sister?' a neighbour managed to whisper to me, her face covered in sweat.

No, I was not ashamed because I was not only screaming out loud my solitude but also my despair at being where I was. After endless, indescribable suffering, the Czech physician reappeared, this time accompanied by an interpreter. He examined me again and blurted out a few words to the interpreter who ordered me in poor French to go to delivery room no. 5.

'Where is delivery room no. 5?' I stammered.

'Go down the corridor,' he mumbled. 'Turn left. Door number five. It's indicated.'

I managed to drag myself along the corridor, pushed open the door and recoiled in horror. Imagine a huge, stinking room, ablaze with neon lighting, full of half-naked women writhing on their beds in silence. Some of them losing blood, some defecating, others vomiting amid the violent barking of the black and white midwives snatching the newborn babies from between their thighs and brutally cutting the umbilical cords. The women who had given birth picked up their babies and staggered towards the exit. Some of them were fainting and lying prostrate on the floor.

Nature works miracles, if it so desires, under any circumstance. Shortly after midnight, on 17 May 1961, I brought into this world not an Alexander but a second lovely little girl with a mop of hair and a voracious appetite. Gnalengbè, who was waiting for me behind a door, guided me in her arms to a kind of tiled bathroom, cluttered with pitchers, plastic basins and various washing utensils. Here she rubbed me with a bunch of straw, removing the blood and matter with which I was covered. She then bathed the newborn in a bucket of water. We left the hospital with me walking as best I could.

I fell asleep from exhaustion in the car that took us home.

I recall this birth in *A Season in Rihata*. But given the bestial, even degrading, nature of the suffering I had endured, my pen refused to obey me and portrayed only a doctored version of the event. Moreover, my heroine, Marie-Hélène, gave birth to a son which symbolized a new departure in her life. For me, nothing changed. I continued to live in a barely furnished flat. Yolande continued to stop over every day to catch her breath. At the end of the afternoon, I continued to admire Sékou Touré driving by in his Mercedes 280 SL while the Boulbinet fishermen continued to greet him with joy.

I very quickly realized that this baby whom I hadn't desired, I must admit, but whom I began to love with the same passion I had for her older sister, Sylvie-Anne, did not entirely belong to me. She who was to become the least African of my daughters began her life as a perfect little Malinké. Sékou Kaba, who was in constant touch with Condé, decided unilaterally that she would bear the first name of her paternal grandmother: Moussokoro. I had to beg and cry for him to agree to add Aicha. He fixed the date of the Muslim name-giving ceremony which took place in the villa where he had just moved. On the appointed day, two white-coated sheep were sacrificed. Then an imam shaved the baby's head before presenting her to parents and relatives. Sékou Kaba assigned me Awa as a nurse, one of his young cousins come all the way from Kankan. She only spoke Malinké and carried the baby constantly on her back. After a few weeks of this arrangement, Aicha became profoundly indifferent to me, only showing any interest when I offered her my breast.

But Awa very quickly had her eat a baby cereal made of millet considered to be far more nourishing.

•

## The Conversion of Saul

*Acts of the Apostles*

At a moment when I couldn't have been more depressed, I made a miraculous recovery. One day I woke up and recalled that I was only twenty-odd years old, twenty-six to be exact. I saw that the sun was shining, the sea and the sky were blue and the almond trees lining the beach at Boulbinet were red and green. Although I never stopped thinking of Jacques, it was the same way I kept my mother in my memory—no bitter, heartbreaking regrets at having lost him. My recovery perhaps coincided with the start of new acquaintances and friendships. Olga Valentin and Anne Arundel were nurses at the Maternal and Child Protection Centre. Olga, like me, came from Guadeloupe. But from Saint-Claude at the other end of the island, so we had never met. She was my opposite: headstrong, dynamic, not at all a dreamer, straightforward and able to get on with everyone. Olga was married to Seyni, a Senegalese, whose extreme left-wing party and satirical journal had been banned and who had to escape to avoid facing certain imprisonment. Welcomed with open arms by Sékou Touré, his status as political refugee entitled him to a huge, half-empty villa with a pool and a sky-blue Skoda. Although he managed to get rid of his bodyguards during the day, he could not prevent a dozen, armed militia from keeping guard in front of his gate from six in the evening to ensure his safety.

Olga and Seyni were gifted with a devastating humour and poked fun at everything: the shortages, the wild imaginings of Sékou Touré who now liked to think he was a poet, and the blunders of the aristocracy that his vulgar and corrupt ministers claimed to embody. Their favourite whipping boy was my friend Louis Gbéhanzin who, like Seyni, worked on the reform of the educational system.

'He's a feudal lord!' they reminded me. 'His ancestors paved the way for the colonizers. They're the ones who are responsible for where our people are today.'

Olga and Seyni debunked politics and taught me to consider it as a perpetual source of derision.

As for Anne Arundel, she was French. Mother of two little mixed-blood girls fathered by a Malian, she was the partner of Néné Khaly. This classics teacher, also assigned to educational reform, was one of the first to disappear into the regime's secret jails. He was an excellent poet and liked to read to us his poems.

•

Unfortunately, he never published anything—Sékou Touré didn't give him time. With Anne and Néné Khaly, contestation was no game—it was violent and passionate.

'Our Maternal and Child Protection Centres are empty!' Anne fumed. 'We can do nothing for the children—they are dying like flies. Their mothers are desperate. Yet whenever the president's men have the slightest thing wrong with them, they fly to Moscow for their health care.'

The couple's best friends were two key political personalities: Mario de Andrade, one of the leaders of Movimento Popular de Libertação de Angola (MPLA), companion to Agostinho Neto, the first president after independence, and his inseparable comrade Amílcar Cabral, co-founder, with his brother Luis, of Partido Africano da Independência da Guiné e Cabo Verde (PAIGC). Every time they stayed over in Conakry, despite their busy agenda of meetings with Sékou Touré and his ministers as well as the ambassadors of certain countries and members of the PDG, they always found time to come and share a frugal meal, frugal because of the severe shortages. These gatherings brimmed with gaiety since Amílcar was a sociable person, always cracking jokes. My new friends, however, took advantage of these moments of relaxation in order to lavish me with advice on how to feel more at ease in Guinean society: learn to speak the national languages, change my Afro for braids and wear traditional wrappers instead of trousers.

•

'That's ridiculous!'

'We're not asking you to disguise yourself as an African,' Amílcar joked. 'We're asking you to try and integrate, at least in appearance. Look at Olga!'

Seyni's wife was a peerless model. She spoke Malinké, Soussou and Fulani fluently. She dressed solely in boubous and had herself named Salamata. I began to loathe the word 'integrate'. All through my childhood I had been unwittingly integrated by my parents in French and Western values. It was not until I discovered Césaire and the Negritude movement that I learnt of my origins and began to distance myself from my colonial heritage. Now what did they want me to do? That I adopt wholeheartedly the culture of Africa? Couldn't they accept me as I was, with my strange ways, my scars and my tattoos? Besides, did 'integrate' boil down to superficially modifying one's appearance? Getting by in a foreign language? Weaving rosettes in one's hair? Doesn't genuine integration involve, above all, an allegiance of one's being, a spiritual transformation? Nobody was concerned about my state of mind or, more importantly, about my state of heart, so full of compassion for the suffering of the people around me. More significantly, my new friends 'politicized' me. They patiently endeavoured to make me see their vision of the world. According to them, throughout the planet, a relentless struggle was being played out between those driven by the desire for power and possessions, and the rest. If I became a Marxist, it was thanks to their contact rather than personal reasoning. If they had been the defenders of capitalism, perhaps I would have imitated them. It is true that a kind of sensitivity, I would even say sentimentality, predisposed me to take pity on the 'oppressed' and to hate the cruelty of the powerful. Later, I blamed my parents for their selfishness, their indifference towards the destitute, and swore I would act differently. My new mentors were not only content to denounce the ravages of colonialism, they also stressed the shortcomings of the pre-colonial era.

'Oh no, it was by no means a golden age as the fanatics claim!' Amílcar would reiterate. 'We know all too well there was domestic slavery, the caste system, the persecution of women as well as the many barbaric practices such as excision and the murder of albinos and twins.'

They handed me arduous works by historians, anthropologists and political analysts which, pencil at the ready, I studied seriously. It was then that I learnt of Marcel Griaule whose *The Pale Fox* so delighted me, Germaine Dieterlen, Denise Paulme, Louis-Vincent Thomas and Georges Balandier. Since the only books available in Conakry were the collection of Sékou Touré's speeches or the PDG highlights, we had to order from the small bookstore in Dakar, the Sankoré. The manager, a friend of Néné Khaly's, was extremely accommodating because the Guinean franc was not convertible and all transactions were difficult. I have tender memories of the times when, huddled in a corner on the terrace of Anne and Néné Khaly's modest villa, I reported on my readings to Amílcar. We were engaged in a friendship that could easily have turned into something else. Physically, he reminded me of Jacques who was never far from my mind. But he was much more lively and talkative. The fact that we never surrendered to our mutual attraction was because he was married and a father, I think, and intended to lead a personal life beyond reproach beholden to a political leader.

'If you claim to be a leader,' he liked to repeat, 'you must preach by example.'

As for me, I had suffered so much that I was scared to liberate my heart and so curbed my feelings.

We often spent the evenings at the Garden of Guinea, a nightclub by the sea in Camayenne. The Amazones, a mediocre women's orchestra which was in favour with Sékou Touré, used to perform there. People would stare at us—these famous revolution-aries living it up like everybody else caused quite a sensation. Mario and Amílcar signed autographs. Sometimes someone would ask me for one too, which amused me no end, little knowing that one day I would sign just as many. Like Jacques, Amílcar loved to dance. Watching his moves on the dance floor, my eyes filled with tears.

When the news of his assassination by the Portuguese secret police reached me in 1973, shortly before his country's independence for which he had worked so hard, I was devastated with grief. My entire past came back to haunt me. I blamed myself for my faintheartedness. Why hadn't I been bolder! A little sexual pleasure would have done me no harm in a life as chaste as a nun.

No, those years in Conakry were not my idea of fun. And they became increasingly difficult. As the shortages worsened, the Butagaz vanished. The lucky ones cooked with charcoal bought for a small fortune in the state-owned stores. The poorest had to be content with wood which, since it was never dry enough, smoked and reeked. It no longer seemed correct to burst out laughing at Sékou Touré endlessly reciting his bad poems on the radio or to curse the committees for culture and education for forcing us to teach them to our students. Something more serious was starting to happen. From one day to the next, homes were emptied of their occupants. In Camayenne, a camp had opened where, it was whispered, they were torturing those who had the nerve to criticize Sékou Touré and the decisions by the PDG. Rumours circulated of riots breaking out and being quelled in blood.

The Fulanis were subject to a brutal repression. I have never really understood what Sékou Touré blamed them for. Of being too attached to their traditional chiefs whose power he had tried to undermine? Whatever the case, it was unwise to be called Ba, Sow or Diallo.

It was then that Condé returned from Paris after his three years at the conservatory, and his presence reassured me somewhat. Thanks to Sékou Kaba, he was appointed director of the National Theatre, a grand-sounding title that came with very little authority. All he had was an office at the Ministry of Culture; his salary was even more insignificant than mine. In charge of prospecting the interior for an annual theatre festival, there was no budget from the government to go with it. How could he pay for his travel, lodging and food expenses? In his own way he was a victim, victim of this corrupt, selfish regime, indifferent to the well-being of its people. I would have liked him to protest. Unfortunately, he was weak-willed and never dared to complain. He wanted me to stop seeing my new friends.

'Mario de Andrade? Amílcar Cabral? Seyni Gueye? They're well-known politicians. You have nothing in common with them,' he would repeat.

Obviously, I refused to listen to him and we began to lead separate lives. Having virtually nothing to do in his office, he slept until noon. In the evening, he disappeared and re-emerged only in the early morning, usually drunk. I must admit he found time to go looking for charcoal, chickens and curd. One day, he even brought back some potatoes and, miraculously, some carrots. I couldn't help feeling a deep sense of guilt towards him. A lying, unfaithful and cheating wife, I was not making his life any easier. It was obvious that I too was destroying him.

•

It was then that I met Guy Tirolien for the second time in Africa. He had left the Ivory Coast a few months after me and was now Commissioner for Information in Niger. He came to Conakry on a government mission for Sékou Touré. Royally housed at the presidential residence, whenever his numerous meetings left him time, he would have himself driven to Boulbinet. We would talk about everything, our little island of Guadeloupe, General de Gaulle (in his opinion a great decolonizer) and about Africa, especially Africa. His cultural knowledge was immense and the books he had me read would be too long to list here. However, I quickly realized that on some subjects our opinions differed. Like Sékou Kaba, he was a fervent admirer of Sékou Touré and considered him one of Africa's most deserving sons. When I reminded him of the shortages, he shrugged his shoulders.

'I know, you're lacking sugar and cooking oil. So what? Sékou Touré can be compared to Churchill who could only promise the English during the Second World War "blood, sweat and tears". A revolution isn't achieved without suffering, sometimes unprecedented for the people.'

I told him of the changes in my life and my relationship with the group that had formed around Mario and Amílcar. His reaction, however, was oddly reserved.

'Andrade? Cabral? Be careful!' he said. 'They're politicians.'

'And you? Aren't you also a politician?' I exclaimed.

'Me? I'm a poet who strayed into politics!' he laughed. 'Like Césaire. That makes all the difference. Those people are calculating, cunning and cruel. They could do you a great deal of harm.'

I was stupefied because he sounded like Condé with whom, to my surprise, he got along well. They shared the same passion for modern Guinean music, the Bembeya Jazz group in particular, and often went out together to the nightclubs.

When he left after a week or so I felt an immense void. We met again years later when both of us came back to live in Guadeloupe. He had paid a heavy tribute to illness and had a leg amputated. He was never to leave his lovely house on the island of Marie-Galante, his birthplace, where I often paid him visits.

Since the Boulbinet flat had become too small for two adults and three children, we obtained a villa in the suburb of Camayenne, thanks to Sékou Kaba. It was an extraordinary feat and deserves an explanation. Supposedly to fight corruption, everything to do with housing was also under state control. Landlords no longer had the right to rent their property, but had to hand over their keys to a central bureau, Habitat for All. Also in charge of the scarce state-owned residences, this bureau collected the rents and oversaw maintenance. The result of such a system, in fact quite simple, was perfect chaos. In order to obtain housing, if you were not one of their relatives or friends, not only did you have to grease the palms of the agents at the bureau but the latter also laid its hands on the rents and never made any repairs. Hundreds of families were living in insalubrious rooms whenever they couldn't pile into the home of a relative who was slightly better off. Some were even forced to go and live in the surrounding villages.

The villa we were allocated was extremely modest—three tiny bedrooms, a minuscule bathroom and a kitchen in the garden. Camayenne, however, was known for its magnificent trees—mango, pink cedar, almond and breadfruit which, to my surprise, nobody picked. And yet I wasn't happy to move, for I was going to lose Yolande's daily visits and my friends who all lived in town on the seafront. Sometimes Amílcar sent for me to be driven to Anne and Néné's place in an official Mercedes. But this only angered Condé: 'My wife is not a call girl!' he would shout at the miserable driver.

Shortly after our arrival in Camayenne, I witnessed a scene which will remain engraved in my memory for ever. To me it symbolized the suffering of the Guinean people. A long procession emerged from the nearby Donka hospital. Lines of men in boubous were carrying on their shoulders small bundles wrapped in white which I recognized as bodies.

•

Children's bodies. An epidemic of measles, a fatal illness for the undernourished, had been declared and was taking the lives of dozens of children.

*The Visit*

*Friedrich Dürrenmatt*

Denis, who was now at the local elementary school, was regularly beaten up—he came home every day with a swollen face, his clothes torn and covered in blood. I had to threaten to complain to the principal before he consented to admit the truth—as soon as they left school, the boys would batter and bruise him, shouting: 'Your mother's a *toubabesse*!' Meaning: Your mother's a white woman.

What hurt me was not just that the epithet was meant to be the supreme insult but also that it denied me the status of an Antillean and referred me back to the model my parents had once adopted. Is colour therefore an invisible varnish?

Denis's pleadings prevented me from complaining to the principal but he continued to endure a beating every day.

More than Conakry proper, the suburb of Camayenne functioned like an African village. My friends were right when they said that I stuck out like a sore thumb. I didn't speak Malinké or any other national language. I didn't wear either the traditional wrapper or a boubou but, rather, a collection of shapeless cotton trousers which were the subject of hilarity or stupefaction, depending on the circumstances. At the district committee meetings, when we were told to keep our neighbourhoods clean by weeding the embankments of Guinea grass, by sweeping and burning the dead leaves and making compost out of them, the assembly was so preoccupied with laughing at me that it paid little attention to the speeches of the commissioners for human investment. It didn't need much imagination to depict the character of Thécla in my novel *En attendant la montée des eaux* and the reactions she provoked from the population of Tiguri. I didn't have her blue eyes and nor would anyone in Camayene have dreamt of burning me alive on a pyre, but nobody thought I was 'normal' either.

It was then that Condé chose to invite his mother to come and stay with us. Although he had often visited her in Siguiri where she lived, she had never reciprocated and thus had never seen the children. We had to find room for her in our Lilliputian home. So Sylvie and Aicha had to share Denis's bedroom while Condé filled the bathroom with strange utensils and a large zinc basin.

Moussokoro Condé didn't look her age. She was tall, slightly mannish, well built and, touchingly, had the same eyes and smile as her son. She did not arrive alone but was accompanied by Abdoulaye, a young boy with sharp, intelligent eyes, whom Condé had fathered well before he left for Paris—and about whose existence I had no idea!

To conclude: you might think that Condé and I were quits, both introducing into the marriage his and her secret little bastard. But it was nothing of the sort. Abdoulaye, born when his father was no more than a teenager, was living testimony to Condé's precociousness and virility. As a consequence, he was worshipped by his grandmother and raised with the conviction of being the only true heir.

Knowing that in every clime the relationship between mother-in-law and daughter-in-law is fraught with difficulty, I had made an effort and prepared myself for the visit. For example, I had learnt the traditional greeting: '*Asalam aleykum*—are you in peace?' I had exchanged my faded baggy trousers for a skirt. I had tied a bandana around my neck like a scarf. And yet it was immediately obvious that my efforts were useless. As soon as she got out of the taxi, Moussokoro affected a kiss and thereafter avoided looking at me. Since she didn't speak French, conversations between us were limited. Over the next few days she ignored me superbly at the same time as she laughed and chattered in Malinké with the crowd of relatives who came to greet her. What did she blame me for? For not being Muslim? For not speaking Malinké? I sensed there was something deeper, that it was not simply the deportation and the Middle Passage that separated us, dispossessing me of my language and my traditions. It was, rather, a question of an ontological difference—I did not belong to her ethnic group, the sacrosanct ethnic group. Whatever I did, I would remain a non-being, excluded from the human race.

The relatives who visited brought succulent dishes, unusual for these times of shortages, indigo wrappers and bottles of perfume. She held court like a queen, seated on a mat spread out on the floor, her feet bare and calloused. Whenever I could, I attended these unending greetings lest Condé became irate; his mother's presence made him irritable and nervous. Not only did he endeavour to satisfy her every whim, dashing to the market, for instance, to buy her kola nuts, but he also tried to appear beyond reproach by giving up smoking his two packets of Job a day as well as the Pilsner Urquell he regularly downed. Armed with an ablution kettle, he would also rush every Friday to the mosque with Abdoulaye.

I could have made fun of all that if Denis hadn't been so visibly upset. The grandmother never let go of Sylvie and Aicha; the former renamed Massa and the latter Moussokoro. She washed them, combed their hair, had them eat with their hands and never allowed them to play, for she constantly clasped them to her breast when they fell asleep. As for Denis—not content to simply ignore him, no doubt painful in itself, she would also order him about in

Malinké which he was incapable of understanding. Sometimes when he stood staring at her in a daze, I was sure she was going to throw her sandals at him, or hit him. Whenever he was present, Abdoulaye would ostentatiously carry out whatever he had been asked to do while Denis choked back his tears in shame.

One day, unable to stand it any longer, I complained to Condé: 'Your mother is being horrible to Denis.'

He rolled his eyes: 'What are you implying? You must admit Denis is somewhat annoying. You're the first to say he is too soft. A real little girl. Look how different Abdoulaye is!'

'I would rather not make such a comparison,' I answered haughtily.

Sometimes, to entertain his mother Condé would invite the griots he had met during the theatre festival. They usually arrived in threes—two singers with a *kora* and a *balafon* player—and then took their seats on our small terrace amid the crowd of neighbours who had come to listen. When their music rose into the air, I couldn't help but be deeply moved, transported by the magic of the sound and the time of day. Against the darkened sky, flocks of bats whirled towards the tops of the trees, silhouetted as if in charcoal on large sheets of grey paper. As though all those I had loved and lost had come back to envelop me and furnish my solitude. I was no longer alone. Rather, I was overjoyed by the presence of these invisible souls.

The end of the concert was followed by a kind of collection, and everyone deposited an offering in a basket that Abdoulaye passed around with a cocky air, the size of the offering depending on the enthusiasm each had felt. According to tradition, those who felt the most would try to stick their banknotes on the musicians' foreheads.

Moussokoro's visit was supposed to last for weeks but it came to an abrupt end. She hadn't been with us for a month when one afternoon Condé rushed into the bedroom where I was having a siesta and announced in a desperate tone of voice: 'My mother's leaving. She's complaining that we're not treating her well.'

'That we're not treating her *well*?' I repeated, dumbfounded.

He sat down on the bed.

'She wants to redo her roof and plumbing. Where does she think I can find the money? I will have to borrow from someone. But from whom? Sékou doesn't have a cent.'

'Can't you try and explain—'

'If I don't give her what she wants, she'll ruin my name wherever she goes. She'll say I'm a bad son, a good for nothing.'

There was a pause. 'She also says you make her feel ill at ease. That you despise her, that you despise Africans.'

I shrugged. We always came back to this, this old quarrel that refused to die. Who despises who? How do we tear down this wall of incomprehension that separates our two communities?

In the end, Condé borrowed some money from a Malinké merchant, a specialist in the black market who purchased essential goods in Sierra Leone and then resold them for a fortune. This disreputable person was to become our accredited lender. Thanks to him, Condé could give his mother what she needed to repair her roof and her plumbing as well as shower her with gifts, in particular an immaculate white sheep that bleated dismally as it was tied to the roof of the taxi taking Moussokoro back to Siguiri. It had arrived just in time for the feast of Tabaski which Moussokoro had no intention of celebrating with us. Because her son had disappointed her no end.

Why?

Simply because he had married a foreigner.

I thought for a long time about the old lady's visit, and I think it helped me better understand Malinké society, based as it was on a series of gestures and mandatory dictates: never smoke, never drink, never miss the five daily prayers, never forget gifts for relatives and visit the mosque regularly. Even though, drained of their original intent and meaning, these gestures had been reduced to nothing more than a series of automatic reflexes. The heart—it didn't count. The fervour with which you prostrated on the tiles of the mosque—that was of little importance. The way you obtained gifts for the family—that didn't matter. Without losing face, Condé could never have explained to his mother that he was struggling with terrible financial difficulties. Such a confession would certainly not have aroused her compassion. On the contrary—it might have aroused her contempt.

But her stay provided me with an opportunity for some serious introspection. Moussokoro complained that I despised her. I denied that I did. But perhaps she was right? I have in mind a photograph taken in the Luxembourg Gardens: my mother smiling, showing her pearly white teeth, her almond-shaped eyes under a grey felt hat. Hadn't I unwittingly compared the two women, preferring the one I never stopped mourning in the secret of my heart? Hadn't I unconsciously tried to remodel Moussokoro along lines which did not suit her?

Condé was visibly relieved when his mother left and he returned to his old ways. He had recently met an Algerian filmmaker, and a musician who lived in a dilapidated dump with two Fulani sisters rumoured to be prostitutes. Lest there be no doubt that they were 'artists', they had let their mops of curly hair grow down to their shoulders and wore strange indigo jellabas. Condé didn't dare imitate their

•

clothes but he did drink with them until he couldn't take it any longer. Sékou Kaba reprimanded him for mingling with the wrong kind of people, unworthy of a decent family man. But I never did. I knew it was a way for him to express his independence and individuality.

Deep down, he was suffocating in Guinea. Deep down, he was dissatisfied, frustrated and unhappy.

Like me.

*The Teachers' Plot*

Meanwhile, the National Teachers' Union was fever-ishly preparing its assembly aimed at assessing the benefits of the educational reform, a reform making little headway. The evaluatory report was to be presented by Secretary General Djibril Tamsir Niane, respected historian and author of the cult book I had read over and over again, *Soundjata ou l'épopée mandingue* (The Epic of Sundiata). Seyni was pre-paring a secondary report and Néné Khaly disclosed little more than the title of his long poem: 'Mamadou, Bineta and the Revolution'.

'It will be a scathing attack!' he said. 'I have placed my criticisms in the mouth of two naive pupils.'

One evening, before dinner, Seyni drove up to Camayenne in his sky-blue Skoda to have me read the text of his report. He was accompanied by one of his sons, Djibril, a close friend of Denis. While the children played, I leafed through the report. I thought it highly technical but not risky. Recommending a radical overhaul of school textbooks, it proposed, in particular, that history manuals devote more chapters to both North African and Atlantic slave trades (something which the Committee for the Memory of Slavery recommended years later for all French schools) as well as African resistance to colonization.

'It's dynamite!' Seyni insisted.

Two days later, during breakfast, the radio informed us that Djibril Tamsir Niane had been arrested, along with many union leaders, most of them, by an odd coincidence, Fulanis. All these people had apparently taken advantage of the teachers' union assembly to conceal a plot, hatched in liaison with a foreign power and aimed at overthrowing the Guinean government. It could have been grotesque, laughable even, if it hadn't been so frightening. I didn't think immediately of Seyni and Néné Khaly. But then I began to worry. I didn't have to teach at Bellevue that day, so around ten o'clock I stepped out to look for a taxi. In Camayenne, that was no easy task, and it took me an hour to find a wheezing, broken-down car. Neither Olga nor Anne was at work, and no one had any news of them. Worried to death, I dashed to their homes, but I could not get near either of them since they were already cordoned off by a line of soldiers.

I could do nothing but go back home to Camayenne.

The afternoon dragged on, filled with the most alarming rumours. No one seemed to have gone to work, and the streets were full of small groups of people, huddled and whispering.

'It's none of your business.' Condé grumbled as I lay awake all night long, 'Your business is to look after the children!'

The next morning, the news bulletins announced that the students at the Donka lycée, where Niane was principal, a beloved and respected principal, had gone on strike, protesting his arrest. The day after, in solidarity, schools throughout the country, even those in the most remote corners, followed suit.

When I arrived at the Bellevue college, the girls had assembled in the yard and refused to go to class even though the bell had rung. Yet our pupils were no rebels, especially the little sixth graders, and it only needed Madame Batchily's urging to persuade most of them to return to class. Only about twenty of the older eighth graders remained outside and, as an act of rebellion, threw stones at the mangoes and then sat down under the trees to eat them. Nothing much to worry about there!

But around ten o'clock, the college gates crashed open and trucks full of armed soldiers charged into the yard. Within moments, the men leapt out of the vehicles and pounced on the young girls. Terrified, the girls began to run in all directions but the soldiers caught them, threw them to the ground and then began to hit them unrelentingly with their rifle butts.

I had never witnessed such a show of savagery.

I have described these scenes in *Heremakhonon* but portrayed Birame III, the hero of the arrested students as Veronica's favourite. In fact Birame III was an extremely intelligent and interested young boy, the son of a physician I often met at Olga's and Seyni's. Every time we met, we discussed the revolution. He was taken to a camp where he was tortured and beaten but managed to escape. I met him again, years later, in Dakar, at the home of Olga and Seyni who had finally left Moscow. He had become a physician like his father, but was now a conventional bourgeois and spoke of his militant past as an error of his youth.

The facts I relate are known as 'the teachers' plot'. It is a pity that they have got so little attention, for they represent the first large-scale crime organized by Sékou Touré's regime. It was a genuine purge which attempted to eliminate not only the Fulani enemy but also the patriots. Some of the schoolchildren were killed, others jailed for months. Hundreds of citizens were tortured, hundreds others forced into exile.

What had become of my friends?

After days of anguish, a Mercedes from the Presidency brought me a message from Amílcar: Seyni, Olga and their three children were safe and sound and had been deported to . . . Russia. Unfortunately, Néné Khaly had been arrested. Anne and his two daughters had fled to Dakar. Anxious to know more, I had myself driven one morning to Hotel Camayenne where Mario and Amílcar usually stayed. There must have been an important political meeting underway—the hotel was full of Arabs, some wearing keffiyehs, but Mario and Amílcar were nowhere to be seen. I was never to see them again in Guinea even though the Single Party rag made no mystery of their visits under the heading 'Personalities Present in Conakry Today'.

Why did they never try to see me again?

Years later, Mario and I worked in the offices of the august establishment of *Présence Africaine*. Since Mario was then concerned with convincing his partner, filmmaker Sarah Maldoror, that nothing had gone on between us, we never referred back to those times.

The teachers' plot unleashed paranoia through-out the country. Once we dreaded the shortages, now we feared for our lives. We were at the mercy of a cruel and unpredictable regime. Everyone kept an eye open for the countless dark-brown police cars always on their rounds, like enormous cockroaches. Where were they going? Who was inside?

Aware of my sharp change of attitude towards the regime, Sékou Kaba tried to convince me that there had in fact been a plot, that the arrests of the union leaders as well as the numerous expulsions had been justified.

As for Condé, he never stopped predicting that I would be thrown into prison. Yet even though two young cousins of Olga who lived at her place were deported, I never felt threatened.

*Frantz Fanon Revisited*

An event occurred shortly afterwards that ended up making me unconditionally anti-establishment. On 6 December 1961, Frantz Fanon died of cancer in Washington DC. As soon as the news reached Guinea, Sékou Touré decreed four days of national mourning. I knew Frantz Fanon all too well. Let us recall that, in 1952, after the publication of extracts of *Black Skin*, *White Masks* in *L'Esprit* I had written to Jean-Marie Domenach to protest this vision of the French Antilles. I realized later that I had been too immature, too 'black skin, white mask' myself to understand such a work and that I ought to read him again. So I stayed at home and read all his books. *The Wretched of the Earth* was a revelation to me and left me shattered. Chapter 3, 'The Trials and Tribulations of National Consciousness', seemed to have been written expressly for Guinea, where the architects of the revolution gradually become its gravediggers. And Chapter 4, 'On National Culture', despite Sékou Touré's epigraph, or perhaps because of it, signified an ultimate irony, made the final scales fall from my eyes. Fanon not only took a stand against all kinds of essentialism and demonstrated that black people existed only as such in the eyes of Europeans, he also went further: while he presented culture, the basis of Negritude, was presented as a monolithic bloc, Fanon refused to give it a definition, preferring to insist on its shifting and constantly innovating nature: 'Culture never has the translucency of custom. Culture eminently eludes any form of simplification. [ . . .] Seeking to stick to tradition or reviving neglected traditions is not only going against history, but against one's people.'

How many times have I quoted these sentences? It was thus that I managed to separate myself from Césaire (though continuing to admire his poetry) and became a follower of Fanon. My new commitment, however, did not do much to change my life. To my knowledge, there were no secret meetings in my immediate surroundings. The opposition, poorly organized inside the country, was mainly located outside Guinea. In any case, the myths surrounding Sékou Touré were such that any opposition or opponent was compared to a counter-revolutionary and dismissed. The way *Heremakhonon* was received in 1976 was proof of this: my daring to depict Sékou as the dictator Malimwana was deemed offensive by journalists and readers alike.

Since it had become impossible to order books from Dakar, I borrowed them from Yolande who, together with Louis, possessed a magnificent library: hundreds of volumes in French and English, carefully labelled and catalogued. Yolande would greet me enthusiastically, overjoyed that I had begun to savour again some intellectual pastimes.

'Louis never stops saying that one day you'll surprise us all,' she said.

'Doing what?'

'Writing novels!'

At that, we both laughed.

'You have an undeniable talent as a storyteller,' she said. 'Take the way you describe your childhood in your family of Grands Nègres.'

Yolande was the only person with whom I sometimes talked about myself. Yet during all those years, the idea of writing never crossed my mind.

Condé's situation had changed. He was back in Conakry only on the weekends; he spent the rest of the week up country, organizing his theatre festival. It was an extremely arduous job, not only because he had neither the money nor the assistance to make things work but also because of its very nature. The notion of 'a play' was perceived in Guinea as a succession of musical interludes and dances, interspersed with poetical tirades. Nobody took Condé's directives and efforts at modernization seriously. He did not belong to the family of griots, so his artistic competence went unrecognized and his years of study in a Paris conservatory utterly ignored. In the eyes of Condé, however, worse was that the 'plays' were used as conduits for the general discontent: the playwrights used them to criticize the regime, often in very original ways. Condé, therefore, had to seek protection from patrons in high places. After much deliberation with Sékou Kaba, he decided to try and get Keita Fodéba interested in his festival.

Why Keita Fodéba? Because before becoming minister of defence, Keita had created and managed the African Ballet and helped it build a global reputation. He had vaguely known Condé in Kankan and, after seeing him perform in an amateur show, had even encouraged him to become an actor.

When Condé begged me to accompany him, I refused. Everybody knew that Fodéba had changed and become one of the most dangerous members of the team in power. A ruthless minister of defence, it was whispered that he was the instigator of the idea of building torture camps for the rebels.

If I ended up accepting Condé's proposal, it was once again in the interest of the children. They were growing up wretched, in utter destitution. An improvement in their father's professional career could only mean an improvement in their lives too.

*The Way to Paradise*
Mario Vargas Llosa

So, one Sunday, we piled into the Renault 4 CV we had purchased with great difficulty, from a French aid worker returning home to Angoulême, and set off for the government zone.

As soon as we crossed the barrage of sentry boxes, armed to the teeth with soldiers who savagely examined our identity papers, we seemed to land up in another world. A world of calm, of luxury, of voluptuousness—flower-filled hedges, carefully raked, soft, green lawns, magnificently pruned trees and long, white ranch-style villas. I was so impressed by the effect that the residential neighbourhood had on me that I have described it in novel after novel, from *Heremakhonon* to *Les Belles Ténébreuses*. It was there that I heard the anecdote that I attribute to Big Boss in *Les Belles Ténébreuses*: Sékou Touré had so admired the Amazon forest on his official visit to Brazil that he had endeavoured to reproduce it

•

around his residence, tropical trees and king vultures included. Dozens of gardeners and ornithologists were employed, night and day.

I had seen Keita Fodéba during a performance of the traditional ballet ensemble at the Presidency. He was a taciturn man, stony-faced and silent. His greeting, when he saw us, was lukewarm at best. His wife, Marie, a pretty mixed-blood covered in jewels and elaborately dressed in the manner of all 'dignitary wives', had nothing to say to us either, and so repeated, over and over, the same question with the same hollow smile: 'How are you? How are you?' Fortunately, she did not expect an answer to her question. They were surrounded by the usual mix of parasites who looked at us contemptuously as if we were annoying scroungers.

When we met them for lunch, we also met their son, Sidikiba, the same age as Denis and just as shy and introverted. Usually alone and excluded, you could sense how happy Denis was to have finally found a playmate. Sidikiba owned a fleet of electric cars large enough to accommodate a child of six or seven. From a Land Rover to a Cadillac to a Peugeot van, nothing was missing. Soon they were making such a racket that Keita Fodéba had to raise his voice to announce that lunch was ready.

The simple meal was delicious—local oysters, mushrooms and barbecued mutton melted in our mouths, mouths accustomed to the gritty meat of puny chickens.

But Keita Fodéba was served a plate of palaver sauce. 'He doesn't like all this white man's food,' Marie said by way of explanation. 'He needs his rice!'

'Just like me!' said Condé, ever the sycophant.

He lived to regret it—Marie signalled to a servant, and he was immediately served the same!

Once lunch was over, Condé and Keita Fodéba shut themselves up in an office to discuss the theatre festival while I remained on the terrace with the other guests who were roaring with laughter, talking loudly in Malinké and ignoring me entirely.

I was now used to that.

When it was time to leave, Sidikiba, Denis, Sylvie and Aicha cried their hearts out at the thought of parting company.

'You'll have to bring them back!' said Keita Fodéba, smiling politely.

As soon as we were back in the car, I flew into a violent rage which was unusual for me since, as a rule, we were content to ignore each other and go our separate ways. But that day I had felt deeply ashamed. Face to face with a dictator's henchman, I could only engage him in an insipid and laboured conversation, unable to breathe a word about the cruel difficulties inflicted upon the lives of the people. I was a coward, playing the perfect role of a poor wretch come to beg for favours.

'You would have preferred to insult him?' Condé asked, dumbfounded. 'In his own house? Is that how you were brought up?'

I couldn't find an answer.

To my utmost surprise, that visit bore fruit. The minister allocated Condé with a handsome budget, an official Skoda, gas coupons. Above all, he had the former cinema fitted out for the theatre festival. Condé, who had no sense of relativity, promptly named it the People's National Theatre and began writing letter after letter to Jean Vilar, inviting him to Guinea. Vilar, out of courtesy, even replied to one of these letters and promised to think about it.

'Do you realize,' Condé repeated feverishly, 'how much it would mean to me if Vilar came here? People would take me seriously.'

I had doubts about that. In this country that was suffering and famished, who would bother about Vilar? Did they even know who he was?

Condé and I were going through a relatively happy period. I would have loved to accompany him on his missions up country since I had never left Conakry, but it was wiser to remain at home with the children. Every night, bursts of gunfire could be heard in every corner of town, then the wail of police sirens. Everyone trembled in their beds. I took comfort in spending my afternoons at the People's National

Theatre, watching the groups rehearse. I still hadn't learnt Malinké or any other language. But I managed to appreciate the words and music of the griots and the call-and-response rhythm of the sounds. Soon I was also able to distinguish the sound of each instrument, not designed to accompany the human voice but, rather, to enthrall by their power and singular beauty. I would sit in the last row of the auditorium and, with my eyes closed, listen to the *diély* Moro Kante accompanied by the *kora*. The deafening yells of the griots that could be heard on the radio were a far perverted cry from this art of harmony, filled with moderation. Besides, weren't the griots about to disappear? They were undoubtedly at risk. Taking as an excuse their difficulty of making ends meet now that their patrons no longer existed, Sékou Touré intended turning them into civil servants—in other words, to convert them into a body of sycophants at the service of his greater glory.

Already, a clique in his pay was shamelessly rewriting history and portraying him as a descendant of Almamy Samory Touré, the great opponent to colonization.

Beside his wish for Vilar to come to Conakry, Condé toyed with the idea of Sékou Touré inaugurating his festival.

'Why would you want to bother yourself with that uncouth dictator?' I asked.

'For you he's an uneducated dictator. For me, he's the president!'

•

Sékou Touré never attended the festival, content to send a subordinate and thereby testifying to the little interest he had for culture, no matter what he said in his fiery radio speeches.

Our conversations came to an end when the festival was brutally abolished. Despite the numerous corrections Condé had demanded, the play by a certain Guilavogui de N'Zérékoré, *The Son of Almany*, was considered too critical of the regime. Guilavogui was thrown into jail; his wives and children managed to escape to Kayes since one of them was from Mali. As festival director, Condé had to write frantic letters exonerating himself. In the end, he was not politically threatened but punished—he lost his operating budget, his Skoda and his gas coupons. And we were reduced to passing the time looking for money in order to simply vegetate, since I was no longer teaching at the Bellevue college.

The only person who still believed in the educational reform was Louis Gbhéhanzin who had devised a higher-education programme: students who passed their baccalaureate and then recruited via competitive examinations would be instructed by the best teachers in the country (which, apparently, included me) and specially qualified after two years' training. What should have been a promotion for me was nothing of the sort. For reasons I have forgotten, or simply because of the country's mismanagement and

•

disorganization, the programme was postponed and finally abandoned.

Starting in early 1962, therefore, I was no longer earning any money and waiting for the salary from my potential new job. Unable to survive on Condé's miserable wage, we were riddled with debt. Condé borrowed constantly from the Malinké merchant who in the past had bailed him out. Although Gnalengbè sent food every day, the meals had the bitter taste of failure and stuck in my throat. That is probably why I dislike Guinean cuisine so much, despite my love for African cooking in general. No longer teaching, I was often tempted to remain in bed all day and neglect myself. Only my two little girls prevented me from having a nervous breakdown; they were my sole occupation, since there were no kindergartens or day-care centres in Conakry, not even private ones.

I was amazed to discover how different they were—Sylvie-Anne was obedient and eager to please whereas Aicha was stubborn, headstrong and capricious. It was absolute bliss to watch their personalities develop. As for Denis, since everyone agreed he was a soft 'little girl', I decided to turn him into a 'real boy' and enrolled him in the Revolution's Youth Brigade. On weekends he would swim, play football or go on long rambles in the bush. I could see he hated all those activities but I stood my ground. I had no idea that worse was in store. One day, barely recovered from the ill treatment of his grandmother, he asked me: 'Am I the girls' brother?'

•

'Why are you asking?'

'Because I'm light-skinned and they're black.'

I had known full well that one day we would have such a conversation. But I had not planned on it occurring so soon—he was barely six. I could do nothing better than admit the truth, for the stench of too many things left unsaid filled the air.

'It's because you don't have the same father!' I stammered.

He stared at me with his beautiful brown eyes which immediately began to brim with tears.

'I'm not Papa's son?'

In this respect, Guinea was not that particular. At school, at the dispensary, in the Youth Brigade, everywhere he went, he was known as Denis Condé.

'No', I tried to explain, aware of my cruelty but incapable of retracting. 'Your father's a Haitian.'

'A Haitian!' he cried dumbfounded, as if I had said a Martian.

It was from that moment on that relations between me and my son began to deteriorate and he who was so tender, so sensitive, gradually became a social misfit, a rebel who went through life accumulating bruises upon his soul.

Even so, I was relatively 'integrated' in my neighbourhood. The neighbours no longer came out on their doorsteps to guffaw noisily as I passed by. The children no longer ran to hide in their mothers' wrappers, nor followed me chanting insults. You could even say I had made new friends, less politicized naturally than Seyni and Olga or Anne and Néné Khaly, and less prestigious than Mario and Amílcar. The villa to the left was occupied by a Guadeloupean girl from Sainte-Anne, Françoise Didon, still a friend after fifty years. She lived with René, a French overseas aid worker who claimed he had refused to serve in the military in Algeria and tried to join the Front de Libération Nationale (FLN).

'But they got suspicious!' he recounted bitterly. 'They didn't believe me.'

I took lessons in Fulani, not Malinké, from my neighbour to the right, a young elementary-school teacher from Dalaba whose husband had been arrested during the teachers' plot. One evening, he reappeared quite unexpectedly, only to die the next morning from internal bleeding caused by the battering he had received. It was rumoured that he wanted to kiss his wife one last time before disappearing for ever.

I had also made great friends with two French women: Fanny, and Frédérique who was a painter. She had approached me while queuing up at the state-owned store to ask my permission to paint a portrait of Sylvie-Anne and Aicha whom she thought adorable. I had to accompany the girls for their

•

sessions at her house and soon we became close friends. One of my greatest regrets is that I left behind the pretty picture she had simply titled *The Condé Children* in our villa at Camayenne when we left Guinea.

Condé also beat a hasty retreat several years after me and did not think of taking it with him. I can imagine, therefore, to my mortification the new occupants throwing it out as rubbish.

Frédérique, a fervent feminist, had me read her idol, Simone de Beauvoir, with whom I was not too familiar. Yet Frédérique was the fourth wife of a polygamist who lived close by with his three other wives. When I expressed surprise at this contradiction, she flew into a rage: 'Oumar never asks me to do the chores of keeping house, doing the laundry or cooking for him. We see each other solely for our pleasure and whenever we feel like it. I raise the daughter I had with him as I like. I'm accountable to no one. I'm free.'

'So,' I joked, 'according to you, polygamy equals women's liberation?'

'At least I have managed to make you laugh,' she retorted.

Indeed, I had learnt neither to laugh nor to smile. What could possibly occur in my life to change my behaviour? My days were lugubrious.

Sometimes I took my children on a picnic to the islands of Loos, accompanied by Gillette who had settled in Conakry in early 1962. Together with Jean, they had formed a couple very much in the public eye. They entertained the upper crust of society in their elegant villa, but, naturally, neither Condé nor I were ever invited to those parties.

Then the catastrophe occurred that put an end to this harmony. It was revealed that Jean was not a physician—expelled from the Faculty of Medicine in Paris, he had made do as a nurse. It was a huge scandal, although rapidly covered up. Given his family connections, Jean managed to find a new job as director of the Patrice Lumumba printing works, an important position since the works printed all of the regime's propaganda. Soon, Jean was driving around in a Chevrolet Impala, a cigar in his mouth and giving orders to dozens of employees. Gillette, however, regarded it as a humiliation. As a result, we became closer.

The islands of Loos formed a paradisiacal string of islands a stone's throw from Conakry. Their beaches of white sand were dotted with leaning coconut palms fit for a picture postcard. You had to make a dash for the ferries which were always full of women and children, families of Russian aid workers with eyes as blue as the sea and the sky. As strange as it may seem from a native of Guadeloupe, it was only then that I discovered the exhilaration of the open sea. Like I have written in *Tales from the Heart*, a bathing suit was a much later addition to my wardrobe. All that blue intoxicated me; I was in seventh heaven. Once, lying on my inflatable mattress, I let myself drift so far out that some fishermen had to drag me back to the shore.

'Be careful the next time!' they advised me as they walked away.

When she was on the islands Gillette never went swimming. Having learnt from her recent tribulations, she instead complained endlessly about the Africans and Africa. I didn't know what to say. I didn't hate Africa. I knew that Africa would never accept me as I was. And yet I didn't blame Africa for my problems, all of which were the consequences of personal decisions. Rather, what tortured me was that I couldn't figure Africa out. Too many contradictory images stacked up one after the other. You never knew which one should have preference: the complex and ageless one of the ethnologists; the one spiritualized to excess by the Negritude movement; the image of suffering and oppression by my revolutionary friends; or the one ripe for carving up by Sékou Touré and his clique.

So, like Diogenes looking for an honest man at the gates of Athens, I would have liked to arm myself with a lamp and run, shouting: 'Africa, where are you?'

*'We'll Go to the Woods No More,*
*The Laurels Have Been Cut'*
Children's Song

At the start of the rainy season, I fell ill. Very ill. I had fainting fits. I couldn't keep anything down. Condé came up with the usual explanation—malaria. But I knew from experience that malaria often hides something quite different. So I insisted on a doctor's opinion, this time a German physician. He who made the same diagnosis as his Polish colleague two years earlier—I was pregnant.

'You are suffering from the most wonderful of illnesses,' he said in excellent French. 'You are going to perpetuate life.'

I was dumbfounded. And so was Condé. We were close to believing in the untimely workings of the Holy Ghost, since our physical relations were non-existent. When exactly had we made love? To make love presupposes either tenderness or desire. We felt neither. Condé spent most of his nights out.

•

When he came home, we would sleep back to back, without touching each other. Mornings, I would wake up and he would still be asleep.

Paradoxically, this fourth pregnancy, so unexpected, so incredible, whipped up my energy and aroused in me a brand-new determination. I realized I had to leave Guinea while there was still time, while I was still young. I realized above all that I had to leave Condé. I couldn't help comparing him to my father. Auguste Boucolon too had been born into poverty. But thanks to his determination and his intelligence, he had achieved a phenomenal social ascension. Condé, on the other hand, was vegetating in mediocrity—and keeping me there with him. I had sacrificed my personal happiness in order to stay in Conakry. I had wanted to guarantee my children a country and a father. But I had miscalculated. The country had been bled dry and the father was incapable of providing for them.

At the same time, and this might seem contradictory, I had no intention of leaving Africa. I was convinced I would end up understanding the continent. It would adopt me and its treasures would make me proud.

In September, I set off again for the college at Bellevue since Louis Gbéhanzin's project was definitely dead and buried.

'Pregnant again!' Madame Batchily exclaimed. (She had only one son, the handsome Miguel, as he was called). 'How many does that make?'

'Four!' I answered apologetically.

She made me feel as if I were a battery hen.

I was back with my students and surprised that the teachers' plot had left an indelible mark on their young minds. None of the girls had forgotten how the soldiers had ill-treated some of them nor the number of students imprisoned or martyred throughout the country. They even maintained that three students from the Donka lycée had been gunned down. Once passive, they had been brutally transformed and were close to becoming rebels.

Among the new staff recruits was a young Haitian, Jean Prophète. We immediately became very close—but nothing sexual this time. Rather, our relationship turned into a sentimental attachment. He described his life, and for the first time I heard the familiar pattern which later was to become so commonplace: the Tontons Macoutes had exterminated his entire family; he had escaped because at that moment he had been playing the piano at a cousin's in Pétionville. Fortunately, he had managed to join an aunt who fled to Montreal and, thanks to her generosity, managed to finish his degree in French.

Jean and I obtained the unusual permission to group our classes and teach together. From that moment on, our classes turned into 'happenings' where, instead of quietly commenting *La prière d'un petit enfant nègre*, Jean denounced the crimes of François Duvalier (I shivered every time his name was mentioned, thinking of Jacques who was perhaps mixed up in all that). Then we introduced the students to the major works of Haitian literature which Jean and I had frenziedly studied together. I can recall how *Governors of the Dew* by Jacques Roumain brought our students close to tears. Madame Batchily not only turned a blind eye to such personal initiatives, sometimes, she even took part in our discussions.

Every day Jean would pedal away on his Chinese bicycle, a 'Flying Pigeon', and come to work with me in Camayenne. Like Guy, he got along like a house on fire with Condé, sharing his taste for music, and for Pilsner Urquell beer.

'You don't understand him,' he said of Condé. 'He's a great guy, a little crazy like all the artists. You're a petty bourgeois.'

As for the children, he adored them and had them call him 'Tonton Jean'.


Keeping in mind the awful memory of the hospital in Donka, I dreaded my return. Eddie, who had finished her studies as midwife, was now practicing in Dakar and invited me to to Senegal instead. I don't know how I managed to get an exit visa, virtually impossible at the time, nor how I was allowed onto one of Air Guinea's planes when I was practically due. Finally, in early March, I flew off to Senegal. My three children travelled with me since I couldn't bring myself to be separated from Denis.

After Conakry, Dakar made an excellent impression on me. The streets were correctly lit and the purpose-built houses were modest but welcoming. And another thing: I was used to the face of black Islam—beggars and cripples crowding around the mosques. Even before I read *La grève des bàttu*, the wonderful novel by Aminata Sow Fall that tells of a beggars' strike, i.e. the carriers of *bàttu* or begging bowls in Wolof, I had understood the overblown aspect of that spectacle, aimed at reminding the privileged, often too quick to forget, that they have a duty—to give to their destitute brothers.

Thanks to Eddie, I was able to rent the first floor of a rather dilapidated house in an outlying district. The ground floor was occupied by a workshop of embroiderers who chanted monotonously while pulling their needles threaded with brightly coloured cotton through the bib front of the boubous.

In Dakar, you are never too far from a mosque and the first call to prayer by the muezzin always threw me to my knees at the foot of the bed. If I hadn't converted to Islam, it's because my friends had repeated often enough that religion was the opium of the people. But I did buy a copy of the Koran; together with the Bible, it became my bedside book.

Despite my lack of money, I liked being in Dakar. The city was more cosmopolitan than Conakry. People were used to strangers and nobody paid me any attention. Moreover, pushing open the door of a bookstore, breathing in the unmistakable smell of books, especially magazines, was a pleasure I began to relish once again. I was excited to read *Ambiguous Adventure* by Cheikh Hamidou Kane whom I had caught sight of as a student in Paris, even though I was more than aware that a myth was being constructed through the pages of that remarkable book. There was no longer a Grande Royale, that's for sure. If she did still exist, she would be deformed by the rigours of postcolonial times, following the brutality of colonization. I read for the first time the pioneers of African literature. But I remained terribly ignorant. I had read the masters of Negritude, but there were also the writings of numerous authors, probably less accomplished, which remained to be discovered. So I began to initiate myself into what they call francophone literature, my future field of university studies. How does the French language metamorphose when it passes through the filter of a foreign expression, in this case African? It was not merely a question of classifying and analysing the unexpected metaphors but, rather, of searching for the inner complexion of the language. Does it change?

But the two most cherished 'discoveries' I made were without a doubt filmmaker Sembène Ousmane and Haitian writer Roger Dorsinville. They have accompanied me throughout my life.

•

It was through Myriam Warner-Vieyra, a friend of Eddie's and wife of Beninese filmmaker Paulin Vieyra, that I met the person who would be my unfailing supporter during the numerous controversies that marked my work. When the Senegalese writers organized a conspiracy against me on the publication of *Segu,* Sembène was my tireless defender. With the presentation of my book in mind, he showered me with recommendations: 'Draw up a list of books you have read as well as your informers, since they will interrogate you on that.'

Then he added, pained: 'Since your Bambara is so poor, they'll say that you never understood what they told you.'

Another ardent defender of this book was Laurent Gbagbo. He was not yet president of the Ivory Coast, merely a young political exile wooed by the French Socialist Party. And a devoted friend. His historian's voice had a lot of clout and he was a constant companion.

Sembène lived in a vast wooden house criss-crossed by breezes from the open sea, situated as it was in the fishermen's village of Yoff on the outskirts of Dakar. While enjoying his fish and rice, he talked passionately about the short film he was working on. (It must have been *Borom Sarret* that was released at the end of 1963, a masterpiece in my opinion and his best film.) He also frequently addressed the tricky topic of national languages, one of his favourite subjects: 'In our cinema, African actors should not be talking in French which is a colonial language that mutilates and misrepresents their personality. They must express themselves in their mother tongue, the one they use and hear in everyday life.'

Colonial language, mother tongue! Later on, I would base my opposition to this dichotomy, which I considered simplistic, on the theories of the linguist Mikhail Bakhtin. But for the time being I dutifully approved. More than a Marxist, Sembène was first and foremost an anti-colonialist. His voice would darken with pain and revolt when he described to me the condition of his father, destroyed by forced colonial labour: building roads, railways and public edifices. His mother had worked herself to death too, raising her children. One of his sisters had been raped by a district officer. He was at a loss for words to denounce that period of humiliation and mourning.

'Unfortunately our leaders,' he raged, 'are the colonizers' best pupils. That's why independence and colonization are so similar.'

I admit I couldn't agree with his virulent criticisms of Senghor. For me, Senghor was above all a great poet. His 'Naked Woman, Black Woman' had taught me to be proud of who I was. He was the close friend of Césaire, the co-founder of the Negritude movement.

I have always had this ambivalent attitude towards Senghor, and I have never denounced his policy of excessive francophilia as I should have.

I had a letter of introduction from Jean Prophète for Roger Dorsinville, Haiti's ambassador to Liberia before Duvalier's crimes forced him to abandon the post, request political asylum in Senegal and thereafter devote his life to literature. He lived in a small, modest house in the suburbs of Dakar. As soon as we met, we felt a great affection for each other. Roger was like the father I never had. Whatever the time of day I visited, I would find him sitting behind his typewriter, filling page after page. I marvelled at that passion for writing which, although I didn't know it, would soon possess me too. I would help myself to a bowl of coffee, sit in an armchair stuffed with threadbare cushions and wait until he had time for me.

It was at Roger's home that I met many Haitian exiles, including the great poet Jean Brière, so courteous and affable. Their company taught me to compare the fate of Haiti with that of the African countries for they both suffered from the same scourge—the negligence and tyranny of leaders indifferent to the fate of their people, widespread corruption and interference from Western countries who had only their own interests at heart. Sometimes I was tempted to confide in Roger about the painful events of my life which had been so important to me. Had he heard of the journalist Jean Dominique? Did he know that Duvalier had an illegitimate son? Was the son working with the government? In short, did he have blood on his hands?

Each time, the absurd nature of such a confession held me back.

•

In Dakar, I saw Anne again who was starting to lose her mind. As thin as a rake, all skin and bones, her eyes inflamed, she kept repeating the same preposterous theory: Sékou Touré was jealous of Néné Khaly's talent as a poet and had him beaten to death by his jailers who then threw his body into a common grave.

'How do you know that?' I asked.

'From the testimony of one of the reformed jailers who escaped to Ziguinchor in the Casamance.'

I must have looked doubtful because she proposed taking me along to meet him in Ziguinchor.

In the end, we dreamt up a thousand projects, but we never went to Ziguinchor and I never met the 'reformed jailer'.

On 24 March 1963, at Le Dantec hospital, I gave birth without a hitch to a delicate, pale baby I named Leila. Because of my poor diet and the shortages in Conakry, my breasts remained empty—I had to bottle-feed her. Leila is my only child I haven't breastfed. As a result, I had to wrestle constantly with the impression that I was losing her.

But the question Eddie and I kept coming back to once I had finished for the day and the children were in bed was: Should I leave Condé or not? Eddie readily acknowledged that the marriage was a disaster. Wouldn't I do better to return to Guadeloupe?

The sad fact was that I no longer had a family to help me. But since Guadeloupe was an overseas department, the French social security system could be set in motion for me.

I stubbornly maintained that I wanted to remain in Africa.

'Why?' Eddie asked. 'What do you expect to get out of it?'

I had no answer.

Arlette Quenum, a former classmate, asked me the same question. At a time when so many Antillean girls had married African men, she had married a Beninese medical professor and now lived separated from him with her two young daughters.

'What are you waiting for?' she asked me. 'Your parents may be dead, but your home is Guadeloupe. You know full well you'll never be accepted here by the Africans.'

I launched into a vague argument. Ever since my mother died, Guadeloupe no longer meant anything to me. I felt free to explore Elsewhere. For the time being, something was keeping me in Africa; I was still convinced that the continent could offer me a wealth of treasures. Such as? Arlette listened to me patiently, then shook her head.

'You want to stay in Africa, then stay! You've taken leave of your senses.'

This last remark remained engraved in my mind. Even today it haunts me. I turn it over and over in my memory's eye. Arlette and a good many others accused me of taking leave of my senses. Hadn't I in fact accumulated a number of dubious decisions and choices while stubbornly pursuing my dreams and fantasies? And hadn't those caused my friends and family a lot of pain? Especially my children, whose interest I always thought I had at heart?

•

*'To Leave.*
*My Heart Was Pounding with Emphatic*
*Generosities'*
Aimé Césaire

With my new baby in my arms I returned to Conakry and resumed teaching at Bellevue. I was less enthusiastic now about working with Jean Prophète for I was absorbed by a new assignment—looking for another job. I combed through all the journals at the college's documentation centre. I wrote hundreds of letters of application, to international organizations and various African research institutions. Given the meagreness of my curriculum vitae at the time, my letters remained unanswered. So I lowered my sights and applied to lycées and colleges in every major town in Africa. I think I received only one offer, from an experimental education centre in Bobo-Dioulasso, in the former Upper Volta. After quite a bit of hesitation, I had the good sense not to follow through. I was not ready to give up, convinced that I would soon be blessed with good fortune.

•

And I was not wrong.

One day, I received a telegram with the single word: 'Come!'

It was from Edouard Helman, writing under the name Yves Bénot, future author of several notable books such as *Idéologies des Indépendances africaines*, *Diderot, de l'athéisme à l'anticolonialisme* and translator of Samuel Ikoku's *N'Krumah's Ghana*.

Edouard had been one of the few intellectuals to openly denounce the teacher's plot and storm out of Guinea where, he said, the revolution had been betrayed. While he taught at Donka, he too lived in the Boulbinet block of flats. And it was rumoured that he was a homosexual. Whatever the case, he was known for his difficult, uncompromising character. Like Yolande, he would stop over every day on my balcony to catch his breath before climbing up to his flat on the eighth floor.

It was thanks to Edouard that I came to love Thomas Hardy. One day, he rushed down to fetch a book he had left behind at my flat. 'I was completely engrossed in it!' he explained. 'It's the most extraordinary book I've ever read.'

The book was *Jude the Obscure* and he lent it to me after he finished it. Its context of despair was wonderfully in keeping with my mood. Very soon, I read all the other novels by Hardy.

Even before I graduated with my degree at the sanatorium in Vence, I was a passionate student of

English literature. I loved the poets—Byron, Shelley, Wordsworth and, above all, Keats. Yet you might say that this fascination with English literature had exerted its spell much earlier. When I was around fifteen, a friend of my mother gave me *Wuthering Heights* to read. I remember relishing it, curled up in my bedroom, one weekend during the rainy season. That tale of violent passion, of a love stronger than death, of revenge and hatred captivated me. Its memory haunted me. Years later, I thought twice before writing *Windward Heights*, a Caribbean adaptation of Brontë's masterpiece, but drew courage from Jean Rhys' example, who in *Wide Sargasso Sea* had cannibalized the characters of Rochester and Bertha Mason from Charlotte Brontë's *Jane Eyre*.

It is odd to underscore the relationship tying Caribbean writers to three English sisters living in an isolated parsonage two centuries earlier.

My fascination did not stop with Emily Brontë, and all my novels swarm with references to English literature. Jean Pinceau, for example, in *Who Slashed Celanire's Throat?*, the physician who sews up the slashed throat of the child found on a heap of garbage, is an avatar of Mary Shelley's Frankenstein. The two characters of Kassem and Ramzi in *Les Belles Ténébreuses* are my version of Robert Louis Stevenson's Dr Jekyll and Mr Hyde.

The unexpected telegram from Helman galvanized me but also filled me with a gnawing apprehension. I didn't know much about Ghana. I didn't speak English. And how was I to pay for five airline tickets to Accra? I didn't have a cent and, apart from the Malinké merchants, I didn't know anyone who would lend me money. Didn't I need a nest egg, even a small one, to embark on such an adventure? And wasn't Helman's telegram a little too laconic? Shouldn't he have explained what kind of job was waiting for me?

After mulling over these questions, I came to the conclusion that the main thing was to leave Guinea. Once outside the country, I would see where I stood.

Then, during one of my sleepless nights I arrived at such a despicable solution to my problem that I'm ashamed to admit to it now—I would pretend to let Condé into the secret because I would never achieve my aim on my own. This stratagem was probably dictated by weakness, vulnerability and a fear of the future. Nevertheless, it revealed my scheming selfishness and my profound contempt for Condé whom I had no qualms exploiting.

I went to wake him up. Since my return from Senegal, distrusting our bodies, he now shared a room with Denis. Our bodies could take us by surprise and we couldn't run the risk of bringing a fifth child into this world.

We sat down on the veranda. I remember the moon high in the sky and the air loaded with a soft humidity while I poured out my tale. For their own good, I explained, we had to shield the children from this life, this life which seemed to offer them no future. I had found an excellent job in Ghana. I would go and check things out. As soon as the children and I had settled in, I would write to him and he could join us.

'Do you really want me to come and join you?' he asked.

'Yes, I do!'

'Does that mean you still love me?'

His voice trembled over those words. To my great shame, I managed to cry a few tears and manifest a pretext of sincerity in order to convince him. Couldn't he understand that it was this cramped existence and this toxic country that was separating us?

From that moment on he took control of matters with an authority that amazed me. He urged me not to say anything about my plans to Sékou Kaba who would never allow me to leave Guinea for good.

'For him, you are heaven and earth,' he commented. 'I know Gnalengbè's been jealous.'

All I had to do was to convince Sékou Kaba that my successive pregnancies had made me depressive and that I needed to recharge my batteries in my home country. Although I was the holder of a local contract with no benefits, there was a possibility of obtaining leave for health reasons.

As expected, Sékou Kaba bit the hook and did his best to help me out. And yet on one point he came up empty-handed—since currency-exchange controls were very strict, in order for my wretched salary to be paid in French francs, the Central Bank of Guinea would have to issue a letter of credit. But it refused to do so for reasons I have now forgotten. Endless palavers with all sorts of bank authorities got us nowhere. Since I couldn't leave penniless with four children, it looked as though my plans would fall through. The Malinké merchants to whom we owed colossal sums of money no longer wanted to lend us a cent. By dint of begging, Condé managed to extort fifty dollars from one of them, and I would have to be content with that miserable sum of money until I got to Dakar where I could scrounge off Eddie once more.

In a small community, it is impossible to keep a secret. I don't know how but soon all of Camayenne knew about my departure. The reaction was not what you would have expected. People who had openly poked fun at me or never spoken a word to me now came up to me in the street and begged me with quivers in their voice not to leave Guinea. 'Where are you going? Where are you taking our children? This is your country.' Others brought over palaver sauces, groundnut *mafé* stews and cakes. I was bewildered, unable to understand this U-turn. In response to their interrogations, I swore that I would not be away for long, a few months at most in my home country.

The truth I confessed only to Yolande and Louis. Sadly, one evening, I climbed up the ten flights of the Boulbinet residence to their flat to bid them farewell.

They listened to me, stupefied.

'Helman?' Yolande cried. 'But he's crazy.'

'Are you familiar with him?' Louis asked calmly. 'He has the reputation of being unstable.'

I stammered that I could no longer live in Guinea.

'Why not?' they asked in one voice.

Whenever there was an electricity outage, we had to use an acetylene lamp. We drank ersatz coffee in which the Russian sugar cubes refused to melt. The Czech mint biscuits we had for our meagre tea time were like pebbles. But that was not the worst—each of us feared for our lives. The most harmless individuals would vanish, would be thrown into prison for no apparent reason. And they were asking me why I no longer wanted to live in Guinea?

As I was attempting to elaborate an answer, Yolande continued: 'Think about what you are about to do with your flock of children!'

Louis drew thoughtfully on his pipe, looking very like the portrait of his royal ancestor in the history textbooks.

'It's a mistake to think that the people are *naturally* ready for revolution. They are cowardly, materialistic and selfish. They have to be coerced. And that's what Sékou has been obliged to do.'

'Coerced!' I exclaimed. 'Does that mean they have to be thrown into prison, tortured and killed?'

He looked at me as if I were an unreasonable child. 'You're exaggerating!' he smiled.

•

No, I wasn't. The NGOs estimated the number of dead at the Boiro camp to be 50,000 and as many again at Kindia, not counting the corpses hastily thrown into common graves across the country.

Yolande and I wept as we parted. Twenty years later, an African History Congress reunited us. She had married Louis. They had a son and were living in Cotonou.

A few days later, while I was in Sékou Kaba's car, he said to me sadly: 'Feminine intuition! Gnalengbè thinks we're wrong to let you leave with the children. You'll never come back to Guinea.'

I didn't have the heart to lie to someone whom I loved so much and who had been so concerned with my well-being. So I said nothing, and we continued in silence, both of us plunged in deep sadness.

I was to see him years later in Abidjan where my daughter Sylvie-Anne was living with her husband, Cheikh Sarr. Considered a lackey of the Guinean regime and consequently discredited, he had had to leave the country; Gnalengbè stayed behind in Kankan. Alone, sick and almost blind, he survived thanks only to the allowances he received from his daughters, refugees in the US. Whereas the whole world condemned the crimes of Sékou Touré, he still admired the man. His illusions undiminished, he would repeat sorrowfully: 'Sékou Touré never hurt anyone. I can say he was a perfect nationalist, beyond reproach. Unfortunately, he was surrounded by careerists, men without an ideal.'

On 22 November 1963, while the world mourned the assassination of John F. Kennedy, I boarded an Air Guinea plane to Dakar, the first stopover on my trip to Ghana. In tears. I had wept a lot during my twenty-seven years of existence, but that day my tears knew no bounds. Seeing me cry, my children too sobbed in unison. Condé tried in vain to console me. Silent and sorrowful, Sékou and Gnalengbè handed me green menthol paper handkerchiefs, a speciality from Yugoslavia sold in the state-owned stores.

Why was I crying?

Because I was leaving this ill-fated land to which I was so deeply attached and to which, I sensed, I would never return. More than the theoretical discourses of my friends, it was this country that taught me compassion and the importance of the people's well-being. That taught me that nothing compares to the suffering of a child. And that infused me with a lesson I would never forget—minimize one's own misfortune and give precedence to that of the greater number. I had lost some of my dearest friends here. And it was here that I was becoming a very different human being.

The heir to the Grands Nègres was suffering a radical break.

Physically too, those years severely marked the children and me. Except for Aicha, who remained lovely and chubby, the rest of us were emaciated.

Leila was especially puny and morose. Afflicted with alopecia, Denis's hair was falling out in clumps. Sylvie's gums and lips were swelling with ulcers which brought her to tears when she ate. Given my meagre resources, I also made our clothes, including Denis's shorts. I cut them out from patterns loaned to me by Mariette Matima, a girl from Guadeloupe who taught dressmaking at the college. We really were a motley lot.

The plane had no sooner taken off than a corpulent woman, magnificently dressed and covered in jewels, emerged from the First Class cabin and approached me. She was a wealthy Soussou merchant, a Madame Cissé whom I had seen on a number of occasions in the neighbourhood, driving her Mercedes 280 SL.

She stuffed a thick wad of dollars in my hand.

'May Allah keep you!' she murmured. 'Take that for yourself and your children.'

And that's how, equipped with a stupefying sum of alms from an unknown woman, I began my third African adventure.

The news of Kennedy's assassination had plunged Dakar into mourning. On every public building, flags flew at half mast. President Senghor had decreed three days of national mourning. But what struck me most was the genuine grief expressed by the people.

In the courtyard where Eddie lived, the tenants crowded around the lucky ones who owned television sets in order to cry over and over again at the sight of Jackie, stricken by misfortune in her pink two-piece suit.

'Sometimes God does not know what He is doing,' they sighed.

I remained far from that wave of emotion. I was, I repeat, a Marxist, perhaps with a narrow viewpoint. For me, JFK was merely a capitalist American who in April 1961 led the fateful invasion of the Bay of Pigs against one of my heroes, Fidel Castro. In fact, the general outpouring of distress spoilt a moment I should have been relishing—of running joyfully along the seashore, of rediscovering the taste of freedom after years of wasting away in purgatory.

One evening we were invited for dinner at Madame Vieyra's. Before we left, Eddie, who knew my political opinions, begged me to say nothing that might shock her. I gave her my word but didn't keep it. So dinner ended with a noisy joust with a Beninese called Soglo who was to become president of his country. At the time he was working as a modest international civil servant for the World Bank in Washington DC. I thought him extremely arrogant as he talked complacently about the region economically under his responsibility as 'my countries'.

I was unaware that, in addition to my freedom, I was beginning another type of apprenticeship—I was learning how to express my ideas.

•

**II**

*Woman Is the Nigger of the World*

John Lennon

After a week spent in Dakar at Eddie's, I arrived at Accra where Helman was waiting for me at the airport. To my amazement, he was wearing a flowery Hawaiian shirt, the type of holiday attire that nobody wore even in Conakry. His eyes were shaded by a pair of enormous square sunglasses which he removed to better examine the small troop walking towards him.

'Why have you brought all these children with you?' he stammered.

'They're mine!' I answered, setting down Leila who still had to be carried.

His expression wilted.

We piled into his tiny car and set off for the town centre. Thirty minutes later, amid a hubbub of horns and a confusion of vehicles, we came to a stop in front of a modest block, pompously named Simon Bolivar

•

Residence, apparently reserved for government guests. We entered a minuscule studio on the ground floor attached to an even smaller kitchenette. Clearly, Helman had been expecting only me.

Without taking the trouble to sit down, he pumped my hand up and down. 'I'll pick you up tomorrow morning at nine o'clock to take you to Flagstaff House.'

'Flagstaff House?'

'It's the seat of government,' he explained. 'For your application.'

And he left.

It was eleven thirty in the morning. He hadn't invited us to lunch or for a drink. Was he one of those people who hated children? What were we going to do all day long? In all my life, and there have been a good many moments of solitude, I had never felt so alone. Carrying Leila in my arms, I pushed the other three children out of the door.

I had never seen a town like Accra—colourful, crowded and noisy. No beggars or cripples, no women in rags waiting in line at the water faucets, no old men enthroned in their chairs. Loudspeakers placed along the pavements blared out a frenzied music which I later learnt was called 'high-life'. Frenzied sounds also drifted out of the numerous bars where televisions barked unheeded. Men draped in costumes resembling Roman togas, women wearing voluminous head ties, chattered and screamed with laughter and drank beer after beer. It was Sunday. Crowds coming out of chapel filled the streets already congested with all sorts of vehicles and streetcarts whose sellers cried out their wares—lottery tickets, toys, newspapers, small books in the local language and various strange objects. I emerged onto a vast esplanade crowded with people out for a stroll. It bordered a beach of brown pebbles fringed by a grey, sluggish sea that reminded me of Grand-Bassam. Children ran naked on the beach, young couples embraced and kissed shamelessly while further on older couples fondled and kissed each other just as openly.

After the Muslim prudery of Conakry, Accra seemed to be Sodom and Gomorrah. I have never been able to dissociate that fairly ordinary small town from those images of vice and extreme liberty.

In the middle of the esplanade rose a strange monument—a sort of arch built in honour of Marcus Garvey. I knew how much Kwame Nkrumah admired Garvey, the life force, at the start of the twentieth century, of the American Back to Africa movement of the former slaves.

I explained to Denis, who was beginning to ask questions, what the Black Star Line was—a shipping company created by Marcus Garvey to take African Americans back home.

We lunched on fried plantains and fritters stuffed with meat which the children greatly appreciated.

•

The next morning, before Helman arrived, a pretty young black woman knocked on my door, two little mixed-blood children hiding in her skirts. Her name was Lina and she had caught sight of me the day before. She too had just arrived in Ghana with her son and daughter, political refugees from the Cape Verde Islands.

'Have you heard of Amílcar Cabral?' I asked rather stupidly.

'He's our God!' she replied.

Lina was to become one of my closest friends and introduced me to the closed circle of Portuguese-speaking African militants who revolved around the family of Agostino Neto in Accra while he roamed the world seeking alliances.

'Don't you worry!' she assured me, taking Leila masterfully in her arms. 'I'm used to this. I'll take them to the Marcus Garvey Centre, an outdoor garden for children of the freedom fighters.'

Freedom fighters! That was the first time I had heard the expression designating the many political refugees welcomed by Ghana which was preparing for the requisite socialist revolution, alone capable of putting an end to the neocolonial noose round Africa's neck.

As agreed, Helman arrived on the dot and took me to Flagstaff House. The seat of government was located on a hill, housing a vast maze of offices, courtyards and corridors. Seated under a huge colour photograph of Nkrumah, Kweku Boateng, a finicky and sullen civil servant, put me through a tough test of my political training and achievements in Guinea. Since I had nothing to show to my credit, he required Helman to be my 'revolutionary guarantor', then placed in front of him a pile of forms which Helman had to sign. And he did, though with little enthusiasm.

'When do I start?' I asked, once we were outside.

'Probably in January,' he mumbled. 'Your file will be vetted by a commission at the start of the year.'

January? Could I hold out until then? I thought, mentally weighing up my financial resources.

'And what will my job be?'

He made a vague gesture. 'I'm not responsible for that.'

Disappointed by his unsatisfactory answers, I could think of nothing else to say and we climbed back into the car in silence. Then, suddenly, he suggested we visit his workplace so that he could introduce me to his colleagues.

'We make a great team!' he boasted.

'Where do you work?'

'At the editorial offices of the *Spark*.' Since my silence signalled my total ignorance, he explained impatiently: '*Spark* or *L'Etincelle*, if you prefer, is an important political bilingual journal, dear to President Nkrumah.'

We drove through a jumble of streets to a small ultramodern building located not far from the town centre. We climbed up four floors and entered a series of luxurious offices. He then introduced me to his colleagues, most of them African from many different countries, but also English and American. One, a Beninese dressed to the nines, his neck squeezed into a red polka-dotted bowtie, introduced himself mysteriously as 'El Duce'.

From the very start, my life in Accra was not easy. Given the difficulties of overcoming the most basic problems of survival, the men in Guinea had no time to be predators—they behaved, rather, like brothers in solidarity and compassion. But things were different in Ghana, and suddenly I was exposed to the hunt. The males who made advances seemed to expect and desire only one thing from me. In the street, men would stare at women, weigh them up and call out to them. But given the life I had led up till then, I had never practised the games of love and sex. I knew nothing about the art of sidestepping the issue, nor of pretence and flirting.

I was a novice.

Two or three days after my visit to Flagstaff House, while my children were spending the day at the Marcus Garvey Centre and I was sipping a cup of real coffee (oh, the joys of a forgotten taste), the ring of the telephone pierced the air. In his inimitable and unpleasant voice, Kweku Boateng made it clear that he was giving me twenty-four hours to evacuate the residence where I was lodged. As for my application, there was no question of pursuing the matter any longer.

'Why not?' I managed to stammer.

'Mr Helman has withdrawn his revolutionary guarantee,' he explained gaily. And hung up.

I was stunned. Why? What had I done? Did it mean I would have to return to Conakry? These thoughts caused such a commotion in my head that I fainted, striking my head on the studio floor. I wanted to die. No, it wasn't one of those stylistic devices, one of those sporadic expressions found in novels—I really wanted to die. To put an end to this ludicrous life, so devoid of charm . . . to become an inert corpse buried six feet under.

I don't know how long I lay flat out on the floor.

At one point the door opened and El Duce appeared. I remember how he stank of a vetiver perfume and the pink bowtie he was wearing that day. When I had met him the day before, he had promised to pay me a visit. But what was he doing at my place so early in the morning? I hadn't the strength to give it thought.

'What's the matter?' he exclaimed as he bumped into me lying on the floor.

He lifted me up, guided me to the sofa, fetched a glass of water from the kitchen and made me drink it. Half in a faint against his shoulder, I sobbed out what had just happened.

'Don't worry, baby,' he said tenderly, 'I'll help you out.'

He also showered me with kisses which I didn't have the strength to resist. Then, suddenly, he pushed me over and, flattening me against the cushions, possessed me there and then.

One always imagines rape as synonymous with violence, that the rapist is a threatening brute, armed with a revolver or a knife. That is not always the case—it can be performed quite subtly. I maintain that I was raped that day. El Duce always denied it, claiming that I never tried to stop him (I was quite incapable) and that he was simply offering me the consolation I sorely needed at such a moment.

Yet he remained true to his word and 'helped me out'. That evening he came for me in his luxurious metallic-grey Mercedes (he was a member of the 'Wa-Benza' tribe), and drove me to Bankole Akpata's. Akpata was a Nigerian political refugee, a friend of Nkrumah, a small man with a kindly appearance to whom I immediately took a liking. Divorced, he was raising his son Akboyefo, the same age as Denis. Although he insisted on flirting with me, because he felt obliged to do so as a man, he was never offended by my rebuffs. He listened to me attentively and then asked me, puzzled: 'But why did Helman do this? He is a remarkable man and is thought of very highly by the president.'

I didn't know what to say.

It took me a long time to understand this episode. I saw Helman again in Paris after our return from Ghana. He appeared to hold me in great esteem and even invited me to speak about the Negritude writers in a college far out in the suburbs where he was teaching. I didn't say a word about his behaviour in Accra.

Since Akpata was flying out the next day for a well-deserved holiday (in his words), he let me have the run of his vast flat, equipped with a television room, a games room and a reading room. He also left me his cook, which meant that for an entire month the children and I ate delicious meals from Ghana and Nigeria—*mafé* with crabs, palaver sauce and freshwater fish stuffed with bitter leaves.

It was an odd stay. The days were calm. The children played in the open-air centre, and I curled up in an armchair and watched television. The programmes were uninteresting, neither films nor documentaries but traditional ceremonies or endless harangues by Nkrumah. Nevertheless, I discovered the medium of television and it began to fascinate me. Then, armed with a Harraps dictionary, I passed into the reading room and taught myself the rudiments of the culture of English-speaking Africa, jotting notes in large black exercise books. I relished the work of Edmond Wilmot Blyden from Sierra Leone, amazed that as early as 1872 he had defended the argument of Africa for the Africans. I familiarized myself with the tribulations of Louis Hunkarin, a

Dahomeyan, who had spent most of his life in French jails. Well before my beloved Negritude poets, the Senegalese Lamine Senghor had uttered the great black holler. I learnt the names of the precursors of pan-Africanism, especially George Padmore, the Jamaican, who had such an influence on Nkrumah. Like my heroine Veronica in *Heremakhonon,* I delved into the writings of the latter, in particular *Consciencism* (1964), the cornerstone of his political theory. Although I must confess I wasn't impressed. In my opinion, Nkrumah cannot be considered either an astute philosopher or a serious political pundit. At the most, an astute juggler of shock formulas.

I found the following especially striking: 'Power corrupts. Absolute power corrupts absolutely.' 'Imperialism, last stage of capitalism.' 'Seek ye first the political kingdom . . .'

It was also at Akpata's that I read a radically different work. In 1954, on a suggestion by George Padmore, political advisor to Nkrumah, then prime minister of the Gold Coast, African American writer Richard Wright was invited to conduct a research trip. That trip resulted in the complex and ambiguous book *Black Power*.

Once I had closed the book, I asked myself a question which echoed the comments by Condé's mother on her hurried departure from our house in Conakry. Deep down, way down, in the minds of the long-colonized West Indians and African Americans, whatever they may say, wasn't there still a good dose of arrogance with regard to Africa? An arrogance they never managed to get rid of? A feeling of superiority? I used to have my doubts. Shouldn't I now admit it? Our education is partly to blame. Hasn't it clouded our judgement and vision and made problematic any 'objective' comprehension? I was furious with Denis's classmates for calling me a *toubabesse*. But wasn't I partly one?

Didn't Richard Wright and I remain somewhat 'alienated'?

When dusk fell, everything changed—my intellectual reflections came to a halt, and I spent my time warding off El Duce. He turned up at six in the evening. There was no question of barring him from the flat for Akpata had given him a duplicate of all the keys. As soon as he arrived, he would pounce on me. We would wrestle wildly, like animals, but in total silence so as not to wake the children. Don't for a moment imagine that it was an erotic game in which I took pleasure. I hated him. I wanted to hurt him. I wanted to have revenge and draw blood. Revenge for what? I don't know. I can't explain what he embodied. Fate? It hadn't exactly blessed me.

One evening, what was bound to happen did happen. At the sound of furniture being overturned and objects knocked over, Denis emerged, so tiny, from the games room.

•

'What do you want? Get out!' El Duce ordered him curtly. 'Your maman and I are having fun.'

Despite his young age, Denis was no fool. When El Duce finally left, he came into my bedroom. Curling up close to me, he whispered: 'If he bothers you again, I'll kill him.'

Needless to say, I sobbed the whole night through.

My feelings for El Duce were highly complex. Always dressed to the nines, he was very handsome. And I was susceptible to his good looks. Yet I couldn't bear the idea of him touching me. Once we had finished wrestling, we often went out. He would take me to house parties, the ultimate entertainment in Accra. Men and women downed litres of home-made gin and whisky. High-life music belted out at full blast. Unused to these highly charged atmospheres, I never knew what to do with myself. Moreover, since my spoken English was extremely basic, I couldn't hold a conversation.

It was thanks to El Duce that I met Roger and Jean Genoud. Roger was Swiss, one of the most intelligent and cultivated men I have rubbed shoulders with. He was to play one of those fundamental roles in my life, like a few other men with whom I had neither an amorous nor physical relation. The first of these was Sékou Kaba. I suppose that they represented for me a new-found tenderness, strength and protection that Guito, the beloved brother, gone too soon, had bestowed on me.

Jean was a witty, fun-loving English girl whom I adored at first sight. Roger and Jean liked to think of themselves as patrons of the arts and letters in Ghana. Frequent visitors to their home included popular playwright Ama Ata Aidoo, whose highly successful play *The Dilemma of a Ghost* was performed at the university in Legon; Kofi Awoonor; Cameron Duodu and Ayi Kwei Armah, to mention only the writers. What amazed me was that these intellectuals constantly let fly barbs against the regime, their main criticism being that there was no freedom of expression. Like in Guinea, the single party, the Convention People's Party (CPP), wrought havoc and was full of sycophants and careerists. I refused to believe in their discourse. I had just arrived in Accra and could not yet form an objective opinion.

Since Roger and Jean suffered from not having children, they envied me my numerous offspring.

'It's unfair!' they complained. 'What have we done to deserve it?'

They offered in all seriousness to adopt Aicha whose independent character they liked.

'She never kisses anyone and only says hello whenever the fancy takes her!' enthused Jean.

El Duce also introduced me to one of his numerous mistresses, Sally Crawford, an African American, with whom later he had a son, Razak. I became a friend of hers and often stayed with her in her pretty house in Oakland, California. One evening, when she had drunk a little too much, she revealed that El Duce had often accused me of ingratitude.

'He said you were a real slut!' she blurted.

El Duce had shown up as my saviour. At the *Spark* offices, Helman, who told him everything, had got scared and returned to Flagstaff House in the afternoon to cancel the 'revolutionary guarantee' he had signed for me. Even the date of my deportation from Ghana had been fixed. It was El Duce who managed to grant me a reprieve by substituting his own 'guarantee' for Helman's, although he had no idea who I was. Could he really ignore the fate of a young black woman alone with four children? So he had alerted one of his powerful agents who had helped protect me. Yet I had not been at all grateful to him. On the contrary.

He hadn't mentioned rape. Nor did I.

Ghana in those years belonged to the African Americans, just as numerous as the Antilleans in French-speaking Africa but more active and militant. Fleeing the racism in the United States, they flocked to this land that they were convinced would become the homeland of the black man. Successful writers like Julian Mayfield rubbed shoulders with budding authors such as lovely Maya Angelou and artists such as Tom Feelings who, once back in the US, drew the remarkable series *The Middle Passage* in 1974. Julia, Richard Wright's daughter, held a literary salon. W. E. B. Du Bois had died in 1963 but left his dreams intact, and an entire team was working feverishly on elaborating the project he had devised with Nkrumah: The Encyclopedia Africana.

The African Americans, however, did not mix with the Ghanaians but, rather, formed a superior caste protected by their high-ranking jobs and high earnings.

The more it went, the more I realized that Negritude was nothing but a wonderful dream. That colour meant nothing.

It was at Sally Crawford's that I spent a sinister Christmas Eve in 1963. The African Americans were discussing the politics of their home country, overjoyed because Lyndon Johnson, who had replaced JFK, seemed determined to end the war in Vietnam. And all of them complained about the all-too-slow progress of civil rights since Martin Luther King Jr's magnificent 'I had a dream' speech. A common nostalgia for their native land bound them together. As usual, I was empty-handed—no country, no family.

•

Perhaps in order to fill the emptiness, I began an affair with one of the African Americans present—Leslie, a real Knight of the Sad Face with large, desperate eyes. Not very talkative, he made love very badly. I was thinking of breaking up with him but didn't have the courage. One afternoon, when I had finally made up my mind, I found his door locked—he had left for Detroit the day before without taking the trouble to tell me. Contrary to reason, I was dreadfully hurt. A few days later, he called me in a broken voice to apologize—it was either a hasty departure or suicide. What happened, I asked. He refused to explain. Sally told me later that he had come out as gay and was living with another man.

Did that explain his behaviour?

In 1974, he sent me a copy of his first novel *Native Daughter*. I sent him a long letter congratulating him for it was a wonderful book—he never answered. When I was living in the US, I attended a writers' conference in East Lansing where he was invited—he never turned up. Our relations were definitely placed under an unlucky star.

Akpata came back shortly after Christmas. As I had run out of money and had no idea where to go, I couldn't move out of his flat. And from that moment on it was against his advances I had to fight. He would appear in my bedroom around midnight in his striped pyjamas and try to force his way into my bed. I thought I could protect myself by taking Leila with me, but that did not discourage him. Worse, Leila slept like a log and remained oblivious to our silent struggles.

But in three days he had arranged everything.

•

*Osagyefo Never Dies*
*Children's Song*

Thanks to Akpata, I was appointed French instructor at the Winneba Ideological Institute of which he was one of the co-directors. He stood guarantor for my political commitment, my faith in African socialism and even my morality, and, going by what he said, it seems I was a paragon of virtue. I was offered a generous salary which enabled me to purchase a car, a Triumph, as well as new clothes for my children and me. I rediscovered the pleasure of wearing elegant clothes and slipping on pretty shoes. I was also able to hire a young girl, Adeeza, to help me take care of the children.

One voice did not welcome this appointment, although everyone else thought it a godsend—that of Roger Genoud. He would have preferred to recruit me for the Ghana Institute of Languages which he directed. 'Be very careful!' he said. 'Winneba is not an easy place for a single woman.'

.

I was not unnerved by his comment. Roger could have said the same for the entire country.

I set off for Winneba on the morning of 3 January 1964 and for the first and last time drove very cautiously the 40 miles between Winneba and Accra. Subsequently, I was to become a speed demon dreaded by all. I had bought a driving licence—it was the custom in Ghana where everything had a price. Apart from the swift initiation by an expert, I knew nothing about the mysteries of the car engine nor where to put the water or the oil. Nor had I sat alone behind a wheel. Fortunately, it was a Sunday, so there was not another vehicle in sight. Just a few cows grazing good-naturedly in the fields and goats scampering about. The villages on the way appeared prosperous, clustered around their church. The blackish sea came into sight fleetingly between the huts. I was in two minds about how I was feeling. Of course I felt reassured about being able to raise my children decently. But I was sorry to leave Accra and cut short the friendships I had begun to build.

What was in store for me?

My apprehension was well founded for I took an immediate dislike to the ugliness of the Kwame Nkrumah Institute of Economics and Political Science, also known as Winneba Ideological Institute, located in a former fishermen's village. A few wretched shacks still remained on the beach, cluttered with garbage, but the rest of the place was modern and soulless. The teaching staff, most of them foreigners, was housed in thirty or so unsightly brick pavilions, each with a tiny garden in front, arranged in a semicircle around two concrete buildings, several storeys high, into which the classrooms were piled. There was also a small concrete square housing a dispensary and a supermarket.

The Winneba Ideological Institute, created in February 1961, was the apple of Nkrumah's eye, the achievement of one of his cherished dreams—to assemble in a single place all the devotees of the African nationalist movements, so that they could teach and propagate the common ideals of pan-Africanism and socialism. The type of students varied: one year, classes of indoctrination had been dispensed to the ambassadors of Ghana appointed to non-African countries; another year, the Institute had welcomed a genuine group of terrorists, capable of revolutionary acts.

The most striking element of this architectural ensemble was a gigantic statue of a book-holding Nkrumah, standing in the middle of the square with the same name, for Winneba was the seat of an unbelievable personality cult. At school, before and after class, the students and teachers assembled in the yard and, around the flag printed with the Black Star, solemnly chanted: *Osagyefo* (the president) *never dies*.

•

The institute's bookstore, also named after Nkrumah, sold only the works of the intellectual leader and the journal of the CPP. In the Kwame Nkrumah Auditorium, speakers from all over the world followed one after the other, their discourses invariably ending with a panegyric of Nkrumahism.

Malcom X paid a visit to the institute the day after I arrived. I had hardly unpacked, but I wouldn't have missed such an event for anything. My interest in Black America went back a long way. My mother had pinned up in her bedroom a photo of eight children, doctors, lawyers and high-ranking soldiers, whom she constantly presented to us as our models. 'It's in America that Blacks can show what they are capable of!' she liked to repeat.

My brother, Guito, would poke fun at her ignorance and naivety behind her back. He described to me the horrors of segregation, lynching and pogroms. In order to make his point, he had me listen to Billie Holiday's song 'Strange Fruit' while he translated the words (he owned a remarkable collection of blues records). As a little girl, I realized that the US was a complex land about which you could truthfully say one thing and then the very opposite. Later on, since the Negritude poets were mad about African American literature, I felt the same. I read Jean Toomer, Nella Larsen, the writers of the Harlem Renaissance and Langston Hughes.

Malcolm X was a tall, yellow man who looked like an Antillean. He spoke for four hours, amid a religious silence, of his encounter with Islam while in jail. His moving and powerful narration left most of us in tears.

The following week it was the turn of Che Guevara. My Spanish was too rudimentary to understand him but I found him even more handsome than his famous beret-wearing photograph. My applause brought the house down.

The most spectacular visit, however, was that of Nkrumah in person, flanked by the president of the brand-new republic of Tanzania, Julius Nyerere. Shortly before noon, their Mercedes swept in, preceded by a fleet of vehicles filled with men pointing their guns at the crowd who, in any case, had been kept at a good distance behind iron barriers. I couldn't help remembering the difference between the way Sékou Touré, another dictator, drove himself in all simplicity around the Boulbinet neighbourhood.

Nkrumah and Nyerere represented a couple similar to Don Quixote and Sancho Panza: Nkrumah tall, visibly extroverted, restless, waving his arms, dressed in a flamboyant *kente*; Nyerere squeezed into a dark grey three-piece suit, small and shy. In the midst of thunderous applause and hurrahs and the usual commotion of griots, the two presidents swept into the building where only a privileged few were admitted. I was not among them.

In fact, as soon as I had set foot in Winneba, I realized that I had been parachuted into an Africa totally different from the one I had known. In this

Africa, there was no place for me, for this was the Africa of the powerful and those who aspired to become powerful. The students didn't bother to attend my classes: What was the point, with a subject as futile as French? My colleagues, too busy courting the visiting VIPs, paid scant attention to me. The only person who did was the director of the institute, Kodwo Addison, one of the most prominent political figures and one of the three men chosen by Nkrumah to replace him if the need arose. He hurled himself on me when I met him to hand over my syllabus. We made love on a black leather sofa beneath the inevitable photo of Nkrumah. He was the perfect specimen of a Ghanaian male—muscular, well built, his face set in the heavy mask of arrogance.

What could have remained as a series of occasional encounters turned into an affair. Soon, our trysts occurred with the regularity of clockwork. He spent the weekends with his family in Accra. Back in Winneba on Monday morning, he invited me for dinner to his place every Tuesday and Friday. In his opulently furnished bungalow, a horde of white-liveried servants bustled about. You might think that the meals would be enlightened by a barrage of intellectual conversations on African socialism, capitalism, underdevelopment and its solutions. There was nothing of the sort—the guests were too busy joking, stuffing themselves with food and drink. I have never seen people consume so much alcohol—whisky, gin, vodka, palm wine, even sake, anything was good enough. A regular guest at Addison's table was the Nigerian professor of economics Samuel Ikoku, flanked by his mistress, a pretty Ghanaian journalist. Samuel Ikoku was the only person in Winneba who took an interest in French which he was learning listening to the Assimil method.

He would try his hand at simple expressions to the great amusement of all: 'Hier, je suis allé à Accra.'

'Ce matin, j'ai pris un bain de mer.'

He was surrounded by a boisterous crowd of teachers of every nationality who liked the good things in life. I remember in particular an English historian, always half drunk, grinning like a faun and married to a magnificent Ethiopian girl who had a devastating sense of humour. He was all for ending the monarchy in England, which shocked me enormously. Sometimes, though, the conversation turned to Nkrumah, but always in a playful mode: his mistresses, his smart sayings, his wisecracks about his visits to London as well as the numerous assassination attempts which he constantly escaped thanks to his lucky star.

After downing a lavish meal and gorging on alcohol, the guests would stagger to their Mercedes where the dozing chauffeurs would be waiting to drive them home. Addison and I would then go up to one of the bedrooms on the first floor. There he would slip on a condom, then throw himself passionately on me, grunting with pleasure which always amazed me since I never felt a thing. Then he would moan with satisfaction and fall asleep like a log.

Then I would get dressed and go downstairs. The guards who surrounded the veranda would salute me, military-style. One of them, armed with a lamp, would escort me back to my bungalow, since the darkness was pitch-black thanks to the profusion of trees. Walking home, I would spot the odd glimmer of light in the windows of some of the neighbouring houses.

I would sit on my veranda and ask myself whether it was to lead this dismal life that I had left Guinea and uprooted my family. Materially speaking, I didn't want for anything. My fridge was packed with fresh and smoked fish and all sorts of game that Adeeza prepared with consummate artistry. But intellectually? I had no friends, and saw no one but Monsieur Tehoda, a refugee from Togo, so gentle and shy that you wondered how he could have led an opposition party and endured being tortured in prison.

I began to ask myself whether the intellectuals in Accra were not in fact right, and that I should keep as far away as possible from anything that bore the name of Nkrumah.

I was famished. My heart was famished. My body was famished. Addison gave me no satisfaction whatsoever. Realizing how mediocre my existence had become undermined my courage. And my God, it needed courage. I perfected my English. I continued my initiation into the culture of English-speaking Africa. I immersed myself in plays by Wole Soyinka after having relished a number of very different novels, all condemning colonialism: *Things Fall Apart* by Chinua Achebe, which was to become a classic, and *Jaguar Nana* by Cyprian Ekwensi.

Through all this, my thoughts kept focusing on the toughest of questions: Had I found what I was looking for? At least, I had come to understand the simple notion to which nobody was paying sufficient attention—Africa is a continent, composed of a wide range of countries, each with a civilization and a society of its own. Ghana was not Guinea. Nkrumah was endeavouring to modernize traditional Ghana with the risk of attacking what Ghanaians considered their most sacred cultural elements. Didn't this amount to dealing the soul of the country a fatal blow?

I was also aware of the conflict between Kwame Nkrumah and J. B. Danquah. Danquah belonged to one of those noble chieftain families which Nkrumah hated (and perhaps secretly envied). Danquah had been the first African to obtain a doctorate in law from the University of London, and many saw in him the makings of the first president of the independent Gold Coast. But elitist and perhaps lacking in vision, he was unable to counter Nkrumah's populist charisma and was beaten in the 1957 presidential elections. Shortly after I arrived in Ghana, he was arbitrarily thrown into jail where he died under sordid conditions.

Given my solitary life, my constant reading, my personal reflections and the stream of high-level political figures passing through Winneba, I matured. And I began to ask myself whether I had really understood Guinea. What were Sékou Touré's real ambitions? Why was he incapable of achieving a revolution?

Two weekends a month I left the children in the very capable hands of Adeeza and drove to Accra. I had recovered from my fright and realized that I loved driving. Since the Triumph was a racing car, I hurtled along the road at breakneck speed. Without lapsing into facile psychological explanations, I would say that driving liberated me from my frustrations and allowed me to have my revenge on the constraints that were weighing me down. The drivers whom I passed hurriedly pressed their brakes and showered me with insults. I tore along; around me, the trees, the fields and the houses flew past. For a time I was all powerful, equal to God.

I had my place at table and a guest room at the Genouds'.

They looked me up and down. 'The company of the Winneba VIPs is not doing you any good!' Roger commented. 'You seem more and more unhappy.'

He despised the Winneba clique.

'Poor Nkrumah! Nobody cares about developing and modernizing Africa. His magnificent institute is too busy boozing, feasting and screwing.'

'What you need,' interrupted Jean, 'is a lover!'

Of course I was careful not to mention Addison. Besides, what was there to say? The affair didn't mean a thing.

*Never Two without Three
and the Third Time Is Fatal*

Guadeloupean Proverb

During my weekends in Accra I also spent a good deal of time with Lina Tavares. I accompanied her to those house parties whose frenzied ambience made a change from my long solitary evenings in Winneba. Lina went from the arm of one man to another, explaining that what might seem frivolous was in fact her way of forgetting too-painful memories. The father of her two children was Santiago de Carvalho, a Portuguese planter to whom she had lent her services for fifteen years. He had neither raped her nor got her pregnant by force—she had loved him. I was amazed, even shocked, to hear such a thing. At the time, a mixed couple seemed to me an aberration. Lina burst out laughing when I stated in all seriousness my ideas.

'There is no colour to a man you love,' she told me. 'You love him, that's all.'

•

Santiago had been murdered before her eyes by some other Portuguese who had been irritated by his over-familiarity with the Africans. She had managed to escape with her children and joined the ranks of the PAIGC. There they had taught her to read and write and to become a pediatric nurse. She was now in Ghana in order to escape the extermination of her network by the Portuguese police.

I was horrified to hear that her only intention was to start afresh with yet another white man like Santiago.

'The Africans are no good!' she claimed. 'All they do is cheat on their wives, beat them and eat the household out of all its money.'

Her dream was not impracticable. Ghana was full of white men, mainly English, but also American and Europeans of every nationality, tired, like Roger and Jean, of their country's politics and wanting a breath of fresh air. Sometimes they married African girls.

One evening, around the end of March—I remember it all too well—Lina took me to the home of Alex and Irina Boadoo for the christening of their new baby. They were a mixed-blood couple, very much in vogue, he an architect and she a model who had been on the cover of *Cosmopolitan*. Their splendid villa was crowded with people, and the buffet, laid out in the garden, was taken by storm. I had just managed to find a seat when a man bent down in front of me and asked in such a perfect English accent that in his African mouth it seemed affected: 'Would you be so kind as to grant me this dance?'

It was with this corny question, this supercliché, that my third passion began. It was to be just as painful as the other two although for very different reasons.

The man was Kwame Aidoo. He was a lawyer, a graduate of Lincoln College, Oxford. After practising law for a few years in Chancery Lane, London, he had returned to Accra and was living with Alex Boadoo, his cousin. Physically, he was just the type of man I liked—not very tall, very black, a mop of thick hair and eyes that were sad and sparkling at the same time. He wore his elegant dark Italian Terylene suit with a kind of ostentation, for in Ghana people were judged by their appearances. As a rule, the men dressed like Nkrumah—either in a kind of tunic with four pockets, known as a 'political suit', or in heavy *kente* cloth for ceremonies.

I've already said I didn't know how to dance. I was therefore about to decline the offer when he seized my wrist with a firm hand and dragged me to the dance floor. Unsure of myself, I did my best. Once the dance was over, we found two seats on the veranda. There we spent the next few moments telling each other our lives.

He learnt with horror and amazement that I taught at Winneba. 'You? In such a place!'

I had a number of other things to confess.

'I'm married. But I'm separated from my husband who lives in Guinea.' And, after a few moments of silence: 'I've got four children.'

He was taken aback. 'How many?'

'Four,' I repeated.

He smiled mischievously: 'Nobody's perfect, as Billy Wilder said.'

To use Seyni's expression while describing Louis Gbéhanzin, he was 'feudal'. The heir to the first family of the tiny kingdom of Ajumako, he hated Nkrumah and the CPP clique who, like Sékou Touré and the PDG in Guinea, in their endeavours to modernize the country, sought to eradicate the powers of the chieftainships.

'I'll take you to Ajumako,' he promised, 'and you'll see how devoted the inhabitants are to us. My father is eighty-seven and, according to custom, they have already begun the funeral rites. I shall not sit on the stool—I'm too busy with my work. But my brother Kodjo will be enthroned in my place.'

Such a description added to the magic of the moment. Around midnight, we went up to the bedroom of one of Alex's sons (currently occupied by Kwame), papered with pictures of the newly discovered Beatles who were raising a storm of hysteria around the world, instead of the inevitable portraits of Nkrumah. I was overwhelmed with happiness. My body and my heart had found their language again.

I drove back to Winneba, at a reasonable speed this time, reliving the moments I had just experienced and reflecting on the future. I had to get rid of Addison—it was now out of the question to make love to him. As soon as I arrived in Winneba, I wrote a letter to him which I had Adeeza deliver immediately. In it I told him I didn't want to see him again. It was all over between us.

Why was I being so hasty, so brutal? What was I liberating myself from? The day went by without incident. As usual, my classroom was three-quarters empty, a fact which no longer bothered me. After lunch I had coffee at the Téhoda's.

Around 6 p.m. a black Mercedes drew up in front of my door and Addison stepped out, surrounded by his bodyguards who then stood watch on my veranda. With his heavy gait, he entered the bungalow. 'I want you to repeat what you wrote to me,' he said calmly. 'I want to hear you say it and I want to know why.'

I complied with a trembling voice, despite myself. But he merely stared at me in dismay which surprised me.

'You are not saying why. What have I done to you? What does all this mean? Is there another man?'

I could have said no. A lie has never scared me. On the contrary. I answered in the affirmative. Silent, he held his head in his hands and remained unmoving, thus, for so long that for the first time I wondered what he actually felt for me. Then suddenly, grown older, he stood up and returned to his car.

I remained disconcerted. He had visibly been hurt. I ended up convinced that it was a question of pride. A man as important as he was, who ate at the president's table, could not tolerate being betrayed by a nonentity.

I spent the night convincing myself that I had nothing to be ashamed of.

The following morning, my children had just left for school when a guard knocked on my door. After a military salute, he handed me a thin envelope containing a short letter from Kodwo Addison, Director, informing me that my functions as French instructor at the Winneba Ideological Institute had been terminated. And that I was obliged to evacuate my bungalow immediately and hand the key back to the housing office.

I had received such notice somewhere else too, at Flagstaff House when Helman had withdrawn his 'revolutionary guarantee'. I explained the situation to Adeeza who burst into tears. Dry-eyed, I packed my cases. When the children came home, we had a quick lunch and, piling into the Triumph, we set off for Accra. They showered me with questions: Why were we leaving? Where were we going? What would their Théoda friends do when they found the house locked? Were we never going to see Winneba again?

Roger and Jean were not too surprised to see us turn up at their place.

'What happened?'

I couldn't bring myself to tell them the truth, so I invented a story that, of course, neither of them believed. Jean told me so later on when I made up my mind to confess. 'I always knew things would end badly for you!' Roger had grumbled.


Deep down I was not really surprised. I had always known that I was not in my place at Winneba and somehow I was waiting for the reprieve to end. For that reason, perhaps, I was against Kwame Aidoo taking up my case in court and endeavouring to defend my rights. I had been hired at Winneba by one word of command. Another had turned me out.

Kwame Aidoo, on the contrary, never stopped thundering that Ghana was a jungle fearing neither God nor man.

'I'm ashamed to belong to such a country!'

*Life Is a Long Calm River*
Étienne Chatiliez

Roger Genoud was to boast later that he had played Father Christmas in my life. And Father Christmas he was. Less than two weeks after my eviction from Winneba, he recruited me for the Ghana Institute of Languages. As a result, I was allocated a traditional wooden house with ten to twelve rooms in the residential neighbourhood of Flagstaff House, surrounded by a garden blossoming with rhododendrons and azaleas. I can recall the children's delight as they explored every nook and cranny of their new abode.

'Is this where we're going to live now?

'It's prettier than Winneba,' said Aicha.

I worried myself sick about the children. On the surface they seemed to tolerate the many changes that occurred in their lives. But I had difficulty believing that they weren't suffering psychologically. Who can say with certainty what goes on in a child's little

•

head? All four wet their bed; Adeeza spent hours washing their sheets. They often had nightmares. Denis bit his nails till they bled. Weren't all these signs disturbing? I frantically looked for the address of a child psychiatrist and managed to track one down at the Korle Bu Hospital. Unfortunately, it was months before one could get an appointment and in the end I gave up.

Since Kwame Aidoo was exasperated by the slow progress of the building of his new villa, I suggested he come and live with me. He accepted reluctantly for, according to Ghanaian tradition, a man doesn't move in with a woman.

Surrounded by the man I loved and my children, I should have been in seventh heaven.

Alas, I was nothing of the sort.

Very soon, an obstacle cropped up between us, an obstacle that I would have never guessed—the children. Kwame conveyed to me quite plainly that except for Denis whom Jean Dominique had abandoned before he was born, it was not up to me to raise them. I was making foreigners out of my daughters, alien additions, whereas they had a father and belonged to the vibrant Malinké community in Guinea. In the meantime, proclaiming that the children were stifling me, he decreed a series of rules. First, he fixed up a playroom in the basement in which the four children were virtually imprisoned. No longer allowed access to the living room, sitting room and library on the ground floor, they had to take their meals with Adeeza in a room next to the kitchen. Under no pretext whatsoever were they to come into our bedroom or bathroom, even though Sylvie-Anne and Aicha loved to try out my perfumes, creams and brilliantine. Frail little Denis was named guardian of his sisters and had to supervise their homework and organize their games, especially on weekends when Kwame required me to accompany him to Ajumako.

Ajumako appears in one of my first plays, *Mort d'Oluwemi d'Ajumako*. I liked its strange architecture, its round huts adorned with dried-mud motifs. When night fell under a pitch-black sky, the women hoisted up their triple skirts and danced like furies in the village square, their shadows silhouetted against the facades lit by the reddish glow of the the torches. Kweku Aidoo, the sovereign and Kwame's father, after reigning for twenty years, was preparing for his demise. All day long, and for a good part of the evening, Kwame and his young brother, who was to ascend the throne, received the grievances of their subjects in the palaver house. At meals, there were never less than thirty guests speaking solely in their mother tongue. When I complained that I didn't understand a word, Kwame shrugged and launched into a new version of the oft-heard suggestion: 'All you need do is learn Twi.'

•

Fortunately, he had a sister called Kwamina who spoke a little English. She had married a prince who died shortly after their wedding. Childless, she had nothing to do with her time—she had one servant to wash her, another to dress her and a third to cover her in jewellery. Then she was carried to a litter set up in the courtyard where a fourth servant fanned her as a hairdresser twisted her thick hair into coils. Thus attired, she held out her hand to be kissed by dozens of supplicants.

She was the one who inundated me with legends of the reigning dynasty.

A sovereign ancestor of Kweku Aidoo, notorious for his cruelty and extremes of temperament, was not ready to give up his power even after the traditional twenty years of rule. His high priests begged him but in vain. He clung to his throne and decided to defy tradition by taking a new wife even though he already had over twenty. He had set his heart on an eleven-year-old virgin, despite it being a crime. But on his wedding night, before he could consummate the marriage, he was seized by a strange illness. His doctors could do nothing to relieve his horrible suffering. And he died.

During the day, I couldn't help thinking of my children. Nor could I shake off the impression that I was a cruel mother.

•

During the long holiday, a number of friends came to visit: Eddie; Françoise Didon, attracted by Ghana's reputation as the only African country, according to the specialists, to emerge from underdevelopment; Gillette, crushed by another crisis in her marriage for Jean had gone and done it again—the practising Roman Catholic, son of practising Roman Catholics, was infatuated with a young beauty, Fatou with the Lovely Eyes. Then he married her according to Muslim tradition and, abandoning his family, set up a new home in a luxurious villa in the compound of ministries. He had not divorced Gillette, although he no longer loved her, because he pitied her, now orphaned and stateless.

All these women, so different from one another, had one thing in common—their dislike for Kwame Aidoo.

'If you don't love my children, you don't love me either!' Eddie thundered, horrified at the way he treated the kids.

Gillette bounced back to take a swipe at him, using the worst Guinean insult: 'He's a counter-revolutionary.'

All three urged me to put an end to this loath-some affair.

'You'll regret it!' predicted Françoise.

•

I was quite incapable of following their advice—I loved Kwame passionately. It wasn't just a physical passion like with Jacques. I admired his intelligence and his immense culture. His god, of course, was Danquah, Nkrumah's unfortunate rival, whom he revered as a martyr. 'He was the one who suggested renaming our country Ghana!' he claimed. 'Nkrumah stole his idea.'

Thanks to him, I set to work reading Danquah's book *The Akan Doctrine of God* which, I must admit, proved somewhat beyond my understanding.

Since discovering Césaire and the Negritude poets, I gave little credit to European culture. This tendency had intensified during my years in Guinea since, unconsciously, I had been influenced by the precepts of Sékou Touré and the PDG. I was convinced that we should mistrust the ruses and traps constantly stirred up by the capitalist West. With Kwame Aidoo, matters took quite a different turn. He thought Edmond Wilmot Blyden's concept of Africa for the Africans nonsensical and in the end dangerous: 'Africa belongs to everyone, anyone who understands her and wants to communicate with her. One of her misfortunes precisely is having lived isolated for too long.'

He declared his utmost admiration for JFK whose assassination, if you remember, I had learnt of with complete indifference. He knew JFK's speeches by heart. How many times had I heard him spout: 'My fellow citizens of the world, ask not what

•

America will do for you, but what together we can do for the freedom of man.'

He also admired Gandhi, Nehru and . . . General de Gaulle. He loved music, all types of music. We would wake up, eat and go to bed amid the commotion of not only symphonies, concertos, requiems but also high-life, calypsos and salsas. It was during those years that music became an integral part of my life.

I should also admit that his origins impressed me. Thanks to him I endeavoured to decipher the symbolism and complex functioning of precolonial societies. Reading the works by R. S. Rattray, I discovered the horrors of human sacrifice as practised by the Ashantis once upon a time. Every time the emperor, the Asantehene, died, hundreds of men and women were put to death or buried alive. Horrified, I interrogated Kwame on the subject. He reacted offhandedly and disconcerted me: 'Don't talk like the English who are completely ignorant on the subject. They were slaves who asked for nothing better than to follow their sovereign into death. It was an honour for them. And their good fortune.'

Wanting to know more about these formidable Ashantis, I invited Françoise Didon to come with me and the children to Kumasi, capital of their former empire. She began by making me swear I would drive at a reasonable speed; everyone refused to get into the car with me, Gillette going so far as to say that unconsciously I was suicidal.

As we left Accra behind, we were swallowed up by a forest far more dense than the one between Bingerville and Abidjan. We drove for hours in a penumbra that was both soft and oppressive. Drawn by the glare of the headlights, strange animals emerged from between the massive tree trunks. Others hooted, screeched and chattered. Invisible birds twittered. Overwhelmed by the power of Nature, even the children fell silent.

Asantehene Agyeman Prempeh II had also been Nkrumah's rival and opposed his policy of destroying the traditional authorities. In the end, however, he had been reduced to a purely ceremonial role. I had often seen him on television, a tall, emaciated old man in traditional garb, head and shoulders taller than his very lovely and very young wife, dressed by the top designers. I was fascinated by the contrast.

Nana Agyeman Prempeh II lived in an elegant palace in the centre of Kumasi, surrounded by a wooden colonnade. Unfortunately, we were unable to mix with the throng of visitors of every origin who crowded onto the galleries—the guards forbade us access because of the children. So we ended up trailing through the sun-drenched streets of the little town and ate barbecued chicken in a cheap restaurant.

Around four in the afternoon, we returned to the palace for a colourful show. Draped in his heavy *kente*, his feet protected by enormous, symbolic sandals (for they were never allowed to touch the ground), Nana Agyeman Prempeh II was making his afternoon rounds, reclining on a litter covered with animal skins and carried by porters on their shoulders. He was preceded and followed by courtiers, bent in two as a sign of respect, their faces covered in ash, chanting litanies while musicians blew noisily on their horns and acrobats cartwheeled a thousand times.

The crowd, composed of foreigners and locals, shouted in admiration as the procession went by.

I should have been shocked by such a 'feudal' display, a mortal venerated and assimilated to a god. On the contrary. This scene from another time opened my eyes and enabled me to answer a question that had puzzled me. Individuals like Nkrumah, Cabral, Seyni, and perhaps Sékou Touré and the revolutionaries, who broached Africa and its precolonial past with modern and finally Western notions, such as justice for all, tolerance, equality, not only did not understand it but also did it enormous harm. Africa was a complex autarchic construction that had to be accepted together with its eyesores and treasures; accepted and even cherished, unlike the time of colonization which was marked by the blind contempt and destruction on the part of the Europeans. The supporters of Negritude would err on the side of idealism. They wanted only to retain the defunct splendours they claimed to be eternal. I was so staggered by this moment of illumination that, despite Françoise's terrified protests, I drove back to Accra at breakneck speed.

After 50 kilometres or so, a group of policemen stopped me. Two of them approached the car ceremoniously and saluted me.

'And driving with all these young children!' one of them exclaimed in a reproachful tone.

'Do you know what speed you were going?' the other one asked.

I shook my head: '180 miles an hour.'

'You're at the mercy of a puncture or an obstacle lying on the road,' added the first one.

People badmouthed Ghana's policemen. Accused them of being corrupt, ready to do anything for a few cedis. I didn't dare find out by offering a baksheesh. I was issued a huge fine and paid up. Françoise breathed again. Taught a lesson, I drove back to Accra very calmly.

A few days later, despite this unfortunate experience, I convinced her to come with me to assess the ravages of the encounter between Africa and the West. It was in the forts scattered along the coast that the unfortunate individuals destined for slavery used to be penned: Cape Coast, Elmina, Dixcove, Anomabu and Takoradi. The Ministry of Tourism had recently

•

renovated these stone monsters into four-star, even five-star hotels. They were a great favourite with tourists, especially African Americans. I was shocked by this commercial enterprise just as twenty years later I would be shocked by the exploitation of Robben Island where Nelson Mandela had been imprisoned. Swedes, Japanese and Americans of every colour reduced it to a photo opportunity.

At Elmina, buses spewed out crowds of African Americans. Whereas they had come to venerate the places where their ancestors had groaned before being shipped off into the Middle Passage, they were greeted by the mocking shouts of hordes of kids: '*Obruni* (Foreigner)! *Obruni*!'

In *Lose Your Mother* (2007), Saidiya Hartman deplores this missed opportunity at Elmina and admits she never felt more foreign—not only because of her origins but also because of her attire. And it's true—the African Americans stand out like sore thumbs. You could even say they have a priceless look. Men and women with huge afros, walking too fast and sweating profusely under a pitiless sun because of their polyester clothes, Hartman states.

My children's presence acted like a magnet. In the restaurants, they would make a beeline for our table: 'They're so adorable! They speak French!'

'I can also speak English!' Aicha would reply.

And they would burst out laughing.

*A Short Interval in the Belly of Dan*

The long holiday came to an end and the flow of visits dried up. I then experienced a surprising feeling—the desire to be alone with myself. Calming the tensions and heading off the looming frictions in the family circle was a daily chore that exhausted me. Denis and Sylvie-Anne were both scared stiff of Kwame; his presence turned them into jelly. Aicha, on the other hand, assumed a rebellious stance which often verged on insolence.

'He's not my father. He's not my stepfather 'cos you're not married to him,' she would say in her stubborn little voice. 'Then why is he ordering us about? And why is he living in our house?'

Kwame was fond only of Leila, the youngest; but she did not reciprocate and cried whenever he approached her.

When I told him how tired I was, Kwame advised I take a short trip abroad. Adeeza was very capable. What was I afraid of? In order to avoid any fuss, he would go back to his cousin Alex for a few days.

With a heavy heart therefore, I bought a ticket for one of the cheap excursions organized by the Black Star Line, the national airline, destination Dahomey before it became Benin.

I wrote in *Tales from the Heart* that my parents never explained the origin of the African diasporas. So I was utterly ignorant on the subject. Louis Gbéhanzin's accounts of his family history as well as numerous cultural programmes on the radio in Ghana had allowed me to understand a little more, even if by nature I was and remain more anxious about the present and especially the future than about the past, which might seem paradoxical in a disciple of Negritude. What is to become of our societies that remain oppressed and marginalized? What place will they occupy in a world that is evolving virtually without them? Will they be forever 'subaltern'?

Little did I know that I was to become the first president of the Committee for the Memory of Slavery created to implement the Taubira Law, proclaiming slavery a crime against humanity.

In those years, I knew very little about Dahomey except what I learnt from a brochure on Fon mythology hastily bought at Accra airport.

I boarded at the crack of dawn a plane crammed with African Americans. I was surprised that I wasn't missing my children as much as I thought I would. On the contrary. Being away from them gave me a surprising feeling of freedom. But I didn't have time to delve into the pangs of introspection. A few minutes into the flight, the young woman seated to my left introduced herself.

'Sister, my name is Amy Evans. I'm a sculptor.'

Then she proudly announced that her ancestors came from Ouidah, a small town in the south of Dahomey.

'How can you be so sure?' I said.

She explained what was all the rage among African Americans—in return for a few hundred dollars, one could obtain a certified family tree from an association composed of key historians. Deep down, I wondered to what extent my life would have been different if I could have located the exact place of my ancestors' origin, the Boucolons and the Quidals, on my father's and mother's side respectively. I didn't have time to find an answer because Maya Glover, my neighbour on the right, intervened.

'Sister, I'm Maya Glover.'

Going by what she said, there was no end to the list of innocents conned into the search of their family tree by groups of unscrupulous historians.

The two women argued bitterly without coming to an agreement. Despite their differences, we left the

•

plane the best of friends and took our seats side by side in the bus meant to take us to a hotel in Cotonou. We barely had time to freshen up before having to climb back into the bus and head for Ouidah, to see the temple of snakes. My tourist brochure informed me of the important role played by Dan, the snake. Born from the sacred excrements of Mawu and Lisa, the two founding goddesses of the world, Dan had contributed to the creation of the universe and it was his coils that held the world in balance.

Next to a noisy market overflowing with magnificent fruit and vegetables stood a small mud-walled hut, inside which writhed a dozen or so enormous pythons, as if varnished in black. Some crawled along the ground; others coiled themselves on top of each other while the bare-breasted, bare-footed priestesses engaged as their keeper chanted prayers. Not in the least disgusted or scared, the African Americans reached out and grabbed the reptiles and the horrible creatures opened their sleepy eyes and stuck out their pink tongues. I almost fainted when the frail Amy tried to coil one of the monsters around her body, then seemed to go into a trance with trembling lips and eyes glistening with tears.

I beat a hasty retreat back into the crowded market, and bought some strange fruit simply because it looked so lovely, savouring every moment the forgotten joy of being free.

'You didn't stay very long in the temple!' Amy remarked reproachfully when she caught up with me. 'It was magic!'

Magic? I kept my repulsion to myself and we climbed back into the bus.

The next visit, to the house of an extraordinary character, Chacha Ajinakou, was less spectacular. Chacha Ajinakou, his true name being Francisco de Souza, was a Brazilian who had arrived in Dahomey as a government official, in charge of registering the slaves leaving the fort São João des Ajudá. He then won the favour of King Guézo and became his protégé. Promoted to being the sole agent for selling human livestock, he had continued practising slavery even when the slave trade had been abolished, first by the English and then the French. Long after 1818, heavily loaded slave ships set sail for Brazil and Cuba thanks to him.

Chacha's pretty abode comprised a dozen rooms, cluttered with the most incongruous furniture—armchairs, settees, sofas, tables of every size, chests of drawers and four-poster beds. In one of the sitting rooms, a life-size portrait had pride of place. Chacha was not handsome, but imposing. His enormous hooked nose stuck out like a beak in the middle of his wide, square face, and he wore a black skull cap decorated with a tassel that hung down over one ear. In the vast courtyard of his domain stood the sinister baracoon, the barracks where the captives waited for the slave ship that would carry them into exile.

A few years later, while I was compiling documentation for *Segu*, a historian from Benin told me that the house, the portrait and the baracoon were of doubtful authenticity, most probably fabricated by the Ministry of Tourism. Nevertheless, this initial excursion as a tourist kindled my imagination. The myths, the legends, the description of the tension between the indigenous inhabitants and the Agoudas, the name given to the slaves from Brazil who managed to buy their freedom and return home, illuminate the pages of my novel written twenty years later. Their influence on my imagination was such that perhaps at the cost of coherence I insisted that one of my characters, Malobali, one of the Traoré sons, journey as far as Dahomey.

Our hotel was situated by the sea, on a very pretty beach. As dusk fell, while our travelling companions were swimming, shouting like children, Amy, Maya and I took our seats at the bar, downing many a glass and growing more and more maudlin. Almost in tears, each of us ranted and raved about our partners and shared a string of grievances. To my surprise I heard myself lament Kwame's selfishness, something

I had until then never admitted to myself. We concluded with a common interrogation: Why do men spoil the lives of women?

'Black men,' specified Maya, thus agreeing with Lina without knowing it. 'It's all because of the way they have been educated. Their mothers, their sisters and society in general treat them like gods—they can do anything they like.'

Maya taught at the famous Medgar Evers College in Brooklyn and based her remarks on a sociological rationale which impressed me.

The next day, at the break of dawn, we set off for the former palace of the kings of Dahomey, the Singboji in Abomey. My heart was thumping, for I was about to discover a familiar place—Louis Gbéhanzin, who had grown up there and played football in the string of courtyards, had often described it to me. Since the palace was being renovated, we could only stroll about the main courtyard, take some photos and wander into a souvenir shop where I was fortunate enough to buy a copy of *Doguicimi*, the historical novel by Paul Hazoumé. Thanks to that book, I was able to imagine the palace in its days of glory, when it spread over an area larger than Ouidah and housed around ten thousand people—the king, his wives, his children, his ministers, his corps of Amazons, female warriors who cut off one breast in order to better shoot with a bow and arrow, his army as well as a multitude of priests, soothsayers, musicians, singers, craftsmen and servants of all sorts. In a wing whose access was unfortunately closed that day were clustered the tombs of the kings, each lying in a circular hut with a roof so low you had to crawl in on all fours.

After lunch we were entertained with dances, and a music concert that in my opinion was totally devoid of feeling, performed purely for commercial reasons. Half a dozen drummers dressed in blouses and baggy red trousers haphazardly beat their drums while a group of dancers executed incongruous figures. Despite this mediocrity, the spectators were overjoyed; they applauded loud enough to bring the house down, stamping their feet and shouting with glee.

What did Africa mean to these African American tourists? An exotic change of scenery from a harsh daily existence defined by racism and shackled by the slow progress of their civil rights. In a few days' time, they would leave for Brooklyn, Washington DC or Ames, Iowa, their eyes blinded by the light, their ears buzzing with the sounds and rhythms and their palates drunk with the strange flavours. They would revel in the memory of somewhat barbaric but captivating images, recalling the splendour of the kings long dead and gone, deliberately forgetting their anonymous ancestors who, by the thousands, had lain groaning in the holds of slave ships. I had nothing in common with them. For me, Africa was neither an exotic landscape nor a digression. Rather, it was a perimeter within which I had been struggling for years. I had just read an interview by African American writer Paule Marshall: she couldn't get over how touched she was, while travelling through Kenya, to hear herself be called 'sister' by the Africans.

As if that's all it needed!

The market women, the taxi drivers, the traders selling cigarettes and acid drops in their booths at the corner of Flagstaff House—they all called me 'sister'. In fact 'sister' was apparently just a polite way of saying 'Miss' or 'Mrs'.

The evening before our return to Accra, Amy and Maya begged me to accompany them to L'Oeil, a nightclub where the best orchestra in the country was playing.

'How can you, a black woman, not like dancing?' Amy exclaimed, outraged, while Maya looked at me in commiseration. 'Too bad! You can drink a glass of champagne with us.'

The club was also a lucrative market for sex. In exchange for a few CFA francs, tourists of both genders procured themselves suitable matches. This too was Africa for its visitors—men defined solely by the size of their penises, women by their sex appeal. L'Oeil was decorated somewhat strangely. Hanging from the ceiling was an enormous white porcelain globe. Striped with red and violet venules, it simulated an eyeball and shed beams of light ranging from green and yellow to orange and blue, transforming the dancers into weird alien-like figures.

We had barely sat down before a dozen males in thin, tight-fitting cotton trousers rushed towards us before we had a moment to sip at our champagne glasses. Soon, my companions, delighted at being assaulted in this way, chuckled with laughter, got up to dance and then rubbed themselves shamelessly against those rutting male bodies. I was incapable of imitating them as I had never known how to separate pleasure from love and sex from matters of the heart. In order to make love, I have to be in love or at least imagine that I am. These men had no appeal for me. My friends thus occupied, there was nothing left for me to do at L'Oeil, so I decided to return to the hotel. Turning a deaf ear to the solicitations of a few stubborn individuals, I managed to reach the exit.

In perfect contrast with the frenzy inside, the night outside was silent, majestic, omnipresent. Not a sound except for the muffled panting of the ocean. In the distance, the beating of a drum.

Had the purpose of my trip been achieved? For a few days I had broken my routine. I had 'rubbed and sharpened my brain against that of others'. Now I felt ready to slip on again my convict's uniform.

Although I was never to see Maya again, I rediscovered Amy when I went to live in New York, in 1995. She was living on Staten Island in a house she had inherited from her mother. From her garden overrun with squirrels one could see the Statue of Liberty. Our lives had followed similar paths. During a trip along the Joliba, she too had been struck by the extraordinary beauty of the region. Ever since, she had endeavoured to reconstitute its magic with her often-monumental sculptures. One of them was called *Segu* and had pride of place in a museum of modern art in Spain.

Unfortunately, I have never seen it.

When I returned to Accra, Leila was missing. Adeeza told me that since the child had complained of a pain in her groin, she had been taken to the Korle Bu Hospital where the pediatrician had diagnosed an abscess. They had then admitted her and performed an operation. Everything had gone according to plan. But when twenty-four hours later Adeeza had gone to fetch her, she had been told that as a result of an epidemic discovered that very morning, all the children had been put in quarantine.

I was shattered.

Wasn't this a sign that God didn't want me to be separated from my children?

•

*'When a Child Appears . . .'*
Victor Hugo

A few weeks later, I was called to collect my daughter from the hospital. Leila, skipping with a rope in a yard with a dozen other children, watched me approach but without any emotion. She had completely forgotten her French and almost all her English; she now only spoke Ga, a language of the Accra region that no one but Adeeza understood. This only served to strengthen the relationship between the two, and I languished in jealousy.

Come October, when my vacation in Dahomey was but a distant memory and the tension between the children and Kwame much worse, I received a visit I was not expecting—Condé.

I admit my behaviour towards him had been totally hypocritical. Though I had made up my mind never to live with him again, I continued to send him news of the children and myself. And never openly terminated our plan to get together again as soon as possible. One afternoon, I thought I was dreaming when in the adjoining office I heard his unmistakable voice asking in his unmistakably bad English: 'I'm looking for my wife, Maryse Condé. I believe she works here.'

I dashed out of my classroom. The secretaries did their best not to laugh at him, for he was dressed in black baggy trousers and a striped tunic embroidered around the neck in the Guinean fashion. I dragged him to the cafeteria on the second floor, empty at that hour. There I told him the truth—I was living with another man. There was no longer room for him in my life.

He showed no emotion: 'I'm not surprised. I hesitated before coming here. I know you all too well. You're a liar, such a liar. You no longer love me. You've never loved me.'

At that moment I broke down in tears. Tears of shame. Tears of remorse. I was all too painfully aware that I had used and abused this man. He let me cry without any attempts at consoling me and then handed me one of those horrible brown envelopes from Guinea.

'Here, Sékou wants you to have this letter.'

Poor Sékou Kaba had swallowed my lies, and was overjoyed at the thought that our family would at last be reunited.

'With the help of your experience,' he had written, 'I am hoping you will build a solid future for you and your children.'

'I will not bother you any longer,' Condé said, standing up and grabbing his suitcase.

'Where are you going?' I asked, suspecting he didn't have a cent to his name.

'Before disappearing out of your life,' he continued solemnly, 'I would like to kiss my children.'

We climbed into the Triumph.

'You've got a nice car,' he said. 'You know how to drive now?'

In Conakry I had failed each of my driving tests. 'Too nervous,' the instructors said.

Remembering that, I burst into tears again.

The Ghana Institute of Languages was situated a good distance from the house. I drove at my usual speed, narrowly avoiding trucks, buses and other cars. Condé clung onto his seat in silence beside me.

'What are you trying to do?' he finally asked when we arrived. 'Kill me? Is that what you want?'

The children were playing in the garden. Their stupefaction and joy at seeing Condé again, even Aicha, usually so undemonstrative, hurt me no end. Had they missed their father that much? They hurled themselves onto him, fought to shower him with kisses and tug the goatee he had grown.

'Papa doudou! Papa darling!' Sylvie-Anne was in raptures.

For reasons I have forgotten, Condé did not leave that day. In fact, he did not leave until after a week. After dinner, the children invaded the room he was sharing with Denis, and laughed and chatted late into the night. What were they telling one another? I was wrought with jealousy, and Kwame with exasperation.

'Go and tell them to shut up!' he begged.

When I entered the children's room, their air of playful mischief made me feel guilty—I hadn't seen them so happy and relaxed in a long time.

Not daring to disturb this spirited atmosphere, I just stood there with a tense smile on my lips.

That week was a week of pure hell. I would not recommend to any woman that she share a home with her ex-husband and her lover, for it is by no means a joyful *ménage à trois*. Kwame treated Condé not as a rival or an accomplice but with condescension. Kwame was an intellectual, a graduate from Oxford with a refined English accent. Condé was a wandering minstrel, a common actor. Kwame was a man of noble birth, Condé a plebeian. You might say that in them the two Africas confronted each other. Oddly enough, Kwame's contempt for Condé rebounded onto me, emphasizing the depressing nature of my marriage. Worse, he insisted I ask Condé for a divorce and give him back the children without further ado. He who never had a penny to his name and constantly cursed his clients for not paying him, said he was prepared to pay for the children's return tickets to Guinea.

•

'I'll make arrangements with my bank,' he said.

Every evening he would ask: 'Have you spoken to him?'

I'd stammer that I hadn't, upon which he'd climb into his car and disappear into the night.

Condé finally flew off with a lot of excess baggage. I had packed a trunk for Sékou and Gnalengbè with cans of concentrated milk, powdered coffee, tea, sardines, lard, margarine, tuna fish, mackerels, tomato sauce, biscuits, rice and couscous. I managed to keep from crying when I said goodbye. We were only to see each other ten years later, in Abidjan, where Condé was in exile and looking for work.

Back from the airport and consoling the children in tears as best I could, I found Kwame waiting for me on the veranda.

'I bet you let him leave without saying a word?' he shouted.

Then ran to his car and drove away at full speed, as he always did.

Looking back, I think I can understand him now; then, I was angry with him. He was still a young man; in fact, both of us were barely thirty. He was starting out as a lawyer, attempting a difficult profession, and he had no inclination to begin life with four extra mouths to feed. Emotionally, he was no doubt jealous of the enormous place the children occupied in my heart. But he lacked tact and diplomacy and ended up harassing me.

Unconsciously, an idea was slowly taking shape in my mind—if I wanted 'to do something with my life', as the expression goes, to put an end to the mediocrity I was struggling with, I would have to continue my studies. How could I manage to do so with such a load on my back? If my mother had been alive I would have temporarily entrusted my children to her as Eddie had to do a few years later, by dispatching her son Sarry to Guadeloupe so she could be free to take the United Nations entrance exams. I was an orphan, lest we forget. What recourse did I have then? In my helplessness, I often thought of asking the Genouds for support since they wanted to adopt Aicha. But my terrible little daughter was too dear to me and I never carried out such a plan.

The sojourn in Ghana was a harrowing one. Nevertheless, my first attempts at writing date back to that time. At the Ghana Institute of Languages I was in charge of two classes of about twenty 'advance' students. I did not teach the rudiments of the French language but, rather, initiated the students into the art of translation. I had no experience or training in a subject that requires a solid apprenticeship; translation bored me to tears. One day, in order to cope with the boredom, I compiled extracts from my own readings. It was also a desperate attempt to convey the beauty of the texts.

I no longer have copies of that anthology, but I remember it was composed of poems by Césaire, Senghor, Apollinaire, Rimbaud, Saint-John Perse as well as the *Pensées* of Pascal and large extracts from Fanon and the Bible. Roger was so delighted with it that he had it printed, and organized a book party in the institute's garden to celebrate its publication.

As the Ghanaians were happy with any pretext to drink and make merry, two hundred people crowded onto the lawn.

'And now you're a writer!' Roger exulted.

It was the first time I had seen my name printed on the cover of a book. But I got no joy out of it. On the contrary—it made me feel scared and embarrassed, emotions I feel even today when, during a book signing, I'm confronted with a pile of my novels.

Meanwhile, Lina, I don't know why, was full of admiration and recommended me to the Ghana Broadcasting Corporation. One of her friends, Mrs Attoh-Mills, worked there and wanted to produce a weekly programme devoted to women. Nothing very original, you can imagine; rather, something that's been done over and over again—interviews of feminine personalities on how they managed to cope with their careers, their husbands and families. I accepted

•

out of respect for Lina. Little could I guess how at ease, dare I say how happy, I felt, wrapped in the protective embrace of a radio studio, like in my mother's womb, discovering how other women succeeded where I always failed. I remember a particularly interesting interview with playwright Efua Sutherland.

The series was abandoned after three months for lack of money. But I was hooked and will never forget the thrill it gave me. For years I was one of the stalwarts of the radio programme *Mille Soleils* produced by Jacqueline Sorel for Radio France Internationale.

Attempting to explain my beginnings as a writer, I see only one reason—I regained imperceptibly a certain confidence in myself. Things were not going well and I was locked into obsessing over my failings and shortcomings. Roger and Jean's affection were sustenance for me, a stimulating tonic. They were so convinced of my intellectual talents that I ended up believing in them myself. And I was infused with Accra's exuberant vitality. My classes at the Institute of Languages were becoming favourites with the students and turning into a forum of ideas that was later to become their hallmark.

One day, at the Broadcasting House, I was approached by two young women.

•

'Are you Maryse Condé?' they asked. 'We want to tell you that we love your programmes.'

It was the first time I had heard such a declaration and was deeply moved.

It was then that I had a very strange experience. I was alone, the children asleep and Kwame God knows where. The garden was dark and silent. Suddenly, the present faded away while events from my former life in Guadeloupe, Paris and Guinea, surged up in my mind: Jean Dominique's exit, my mother's death, the 'teachers' plot' and the terrified girls assembled in the yard of the Bellevue college. I also saw Cabral at the Garden of Camayenne, dragging me onto the dance floor: 'The revolutionaries are slumming it!' he laughed.

I would have liked to give these moments a life of their own that time could not destroy. But how?

I did not know.

I believe it was my first inducement to write although at that moment I did not realize that those impressions, those sensations, had to be put to paper.

That night remains an inexplicable and quasi-mystical experience.

•

## 'Memory in Desperate Straits'

*Evelyne Trouillot*

The shrew of life, however, continued to limp along, and nights of passion alternated with days of depression and hours of study when, quite unexpectedly, an event of considerable importance occurred.

Around 4 a.m. on 24 February 1966, Kwame and I were woken by the sounds of heavy gunfire, bursts of artillery and screams. Terrified, the children ran into our bedroom; although Kwame had declared it strictly out of bounds, he didn't have the heart to throw them out. For a few moments we remained silent, clutching one another. Then Kwame and I cautiously ventured out onto the veranda. Everything was silent  But above the magnolias in the garden, the sky had turned orange.

At six o'clock, the television informed us that a military coup had overthrown the president of the republic. For the first time we heard the names of Colonel Kotoka and Lieutenant General Afrifra, the

•

instigators. Dumbfounded, we watched as two young men appeared on the screen, quite ordinary-looking, dressed in military uniform, and explained their act in five words: Kwame Nkrumah was a dictator.

Everyone was asked to go about their daily business. As a security measure, a curfew had been declared and the schools and university closed.

Around eight o'clock—God, how time drags at such moments—the sound of tanks could be heard. Leaving the children with Adeeza and Kwobena, Kwame's young brother who often spent the night at our place, Kwame and I ventured out on foot. Beyond Flagstaff House there was no room to move, and all the neighbouring roads were filled with a fanatical crowd, men and women dancing frenziedly, their faces daubed in white (the color of victory, I learnt later). This human river carried us to the centre of town. There, the statue of the man who two days earlier had been worshipped as a god lay in a thousand pieces, stamped on by a fanatical people.

I couldn't believe my eyes. I was well aware of the growing opposition to Nkrumah. Conor Cruise O'Brien had criticized him in the British press for being aided and abetted by corrupt and materialistic sycophants, caring little for the well-being of his people and disregarding even basic human rights, such as the freedom of expression. Hadn't one of his ministers, Krobo Edusei, acquired a bed made of gold?

•

An increasing number of opponents also blamed him for the brutality of his reforms of religion and the traditional authorities. And above all for transforming the country into a safe haven not only for anti-colonial activists, such as the FLN in Algeria, but also for opponents to democratically elected governments, rightly or wrongly labelled 'puppets' or 'valets of imperialism'.

I didn't really have an opinion. I thought it only right, however, that Ghana was not housing camps for political prisoners. It appeared to me that the people were not lacking for anything, that their standard of living, constantly on the rise, was one of the highest in sub-Saharan Africa.

So why this jubilation?

I remembered Louis Gbéhanzin's words which had so shocked me at the time: 'You shouldn't think that the people are naturally prepared for revolution. They have to be forced.'

We made a stop at Roger and Jean's villa which was full of the usual crowd of writers and artists, but this time in a mournful mood. At first surprised, it didn't take me long to understand why. Gripped with anguish and fear, all these people, like Roger, who had never stopped criticizing Nkrumah, were wondering about the future of the country in the hands of upstarts such as Kotoka and Afrifa.

•

The Osagyefo did not, after all, deserve to be deposed so brutally.

Only Kwame Aidoo manifested his outright satisfaction: 'At long last, the country will be born again! The days of intolerance and favouritism are over.'

Nobody reacted. The Genouds had never liked Kwame very much, I could feel it. But out of respect for me they had always kept their feelings to themselves. It was only during one of my visits to Switzerland, shortly before his premature end from leukaemia, that Roger had said: 'It pained Jean and I to see you with that guy. We wondered what you saw in that self-satisfied little bourgeois. OK, he was handsome. But was that enough?'

What can you expect! One can never shake off one's origins. I couldn't forget that I too came from a family of arrogant petty bourgeois. And perhaps I was not as intelligent as my friends thought. Otherwise, how could I explain such a chaotic life?

As dusk fell, the television informed us that Nkrumah had fled to Conakry where Sékou Touré had offered him co-presidency of Guinea.

'Has he consulted his people on the subject?' wondered Kwame Aidoo.

Once again, nobody responded. This time, though, he had a point.

•

On 26 February, relaxing on the veranda, I was reading a story by Enid Blyton to the children whose school was still closed when, to my great surprise, two police cars and a prison van, a 'Black Maria' (so called because of its strange shape, half-hearse, half-delivery truck), drove into the garden. The doors slammed and a dozen police officers rushed towards me. One of them, visibly the leader, fat and squat and wearing a flat helmet, opened a file, pulled out a form and asked me ceremoniously: 'Are you Maryse Condé, born on 11 February 19**, a citizen of Guinea?'

I was about to correct him: I was born in Guadeloupe and was, consequently, a French citizen. But then I remembered that I owned a Guinean passport.

So I said: Yes.

'Then,' he continued, 'in the name of the provisional government of the republic of Ghana, I arrest you.'

'Why?'

Without answering he signalled to his acolytes who handcuffed me, shackled my legs and dragged me to the prison van. The children began to scream and amid their cries the cars began to drive off.

'Tell Kwame I've been arrested!' I managed to shout to Adeeza who had rushed out onto the veranda, stunned.

•

In several of my novels, from *Heremakhonon* to *En attendant la montée des eaux,* a character is driven away in a prison van. It is hard to forget such an event; the memory of it still haunts me. You imagine your life is over, that you'll never get out of that narrow space where a feeble light seeps in through a small, square wire-meshed window. You imagine there is no longer a future, that freedom and light are over, that you are locked alive in your coffin and being driven God knows where.

It's not fear you feel but a degradation of your personality and the conviction that you no longer belong to this world.

The drive seemed endless. When I was finally manhandled out by two policemen, I found myself in an unfamiliar neighbourhood. I was then dragged to a brand-new concrete building, the Albert Luthuli Detention Centre. In the street full of potholes, cluttered with all sorts of garbage, children were playing football, oblivious to what was happening around them . I felt like shouting: 'Do something! Can't you see what they're doing to me?'

I was led into a courtyard, then forced to shuffle up a series of stairs, all movement made extremely uncomfortable by the shackles on my feet. Then, finally, I was in a windowless cell. All it had was a pallet and on that I collapsed.

I lay in the dark for hours. Just as I was about to pee on myself, the door opened and two women entered, surprisingly jovial and motherly, who freed my wrists and legs.

'That's better, isn't it, baby?' one of them said, smiling.

They were wearing a strange uniform of heavy black canvas, spattered with enormous white spots. A corps of wardens specially created for women, they were known as 'the leopard women'. The one who took me to the stinking latrines told me the charge against me: I was a spy in the pay of Nkrumah who had fled to the enemy country of Guinea. I didn't have the heart to laugh at such nonsense. One doesn't laugh when one is faced with misfortune.

I don't know how but the news had spread through the centre that I was separated from my four young children. As a result, I was soon pampered by the leopard women. The one who pushed the meal trolley dished out a double ration, even though I couldn't eat a thing.

During the four days and four nights I spent there, I also observed numerous aberrations which were typical of Ghana. Money could buy anything. A few cedis, a few pesewas, and breakfast came with a basket of chilled fruit. A few more banknotes and a delicious palaver sauce came for lunch. Even genuine Scotch whisky and not the local ersatz was available if you only had the money for it.

Although I didn't have a cent, my jailers were prepared to give me credit but were dismayed that I didn't want anything. I could neither eat nor drink. I don't know who I missed the most, Kwame or the children. There were moments when I was convinced I would never see them again. At other times, I felt some hope—the provisional government wouldn't be stupid enough to take me for a spy.

On the morning of the fourth day, just when I was at the end of my tether, a group of soldiers entered my cell. One of them announced that I was free. 'My lawyer' he said was waiting for me in the visiting room.

I almost broke my neck dashing down the stairs. Kwame was waiting for me, dressed in his solemn black robe. Red-eyed, he appeared infinitely sad as he kissed me half-heartedly. Why this cold approach? Wasn't I free? Wasn't I going back home? Wasn't our life going to start all over again?

I didn't have time to respond to the ovation of the leopard women, who, assembled in the courtyard, greeted me like a star, because Kwame grabbed me by the arm and dragged me to his car. Inside, he explained what had happened. 'Because of your ties to Guinea, you're accused of espionage.'

'I know, I know. But it's ridiculous,' I exclaimed. 'It doesn't make sense.'

'Perhaps. But because of that, you're being deported from Ghana!'

Deported!

'You have twenty-four hours to leave Accra. That's all I could manage for you.'

•

'That's absurd!'

Suddenly he burst into tears. Of all the pictures piled into the chaos of my memory, I cherish that one in particular—the arrogant, uncompromising Kwame Aidoo, barrister-at-law, educated at Oxford, so proud of his impeccable English accent and his patrician origins, his shoulders shaking with sobs, his face pressed against the steering wheel of his car, crying his heart out because I was leaving.

I took him into my arms like a mother consoling her child. Even more surprising, I remained dry-eyed. I'm not sure what I was feeling. Stunned, I was endeavouring to understand the meaning of those three barbaric syllables: de-port-ed. But my brain was numb.

The short hours that followed resembled somewhat the time when I left Guinea. My house was crowded with neighbours I hardly knew, Kwame's friends whom I had met once or twice, his relatives and Adeeza's family. This time, however, I did not ask myself what it all meant. I understood. These visits were by no means a repudiation of the military coup or the decisions of the junta in power. Even less were they a sign of endearment. Rather, they were a ritual that African societies practised under certain circumstances: when someone departed the country or this life, on the occasion of a wedding or a birth. The visitors were dressed in dark colours, some all in black, their faces sad and glazed. They gave me presents: clothes for the children, high-life records and embroidered wrappers. Kwame's cousins, Alex and Irina Aidoo, arrived at the wheel of their Porsche, she in an extravagant red dress, cut low at the back, and Alex brandishing champagne bottles. Raising his glass in a toast, he declared: 'Kwame is the best lawyer in the country. He'll get you out of this mess. Soon you'll be back with us in Ghana.'

In a way Kwame had already proved his talent as a lawyer, managing to free me after a mere four days of detention whereas my friends Roger and Jean Genoud, Lina Tavares, Bankole Akpata and El Duce still rotted in prison, awaiting their fate. It would be many months until they too were deported.

Amid applause from the onlookers, Alex went down into the garden to spill the traditional libations over the soil.

The Black Star Line plane took off at seven in the morning. I would certainly have gone crazy at the agonizing thought of being separated from Kwame, not knowing whether I would see him again, if an unexpected event, with a symbolic significance in my opinion, had not monopolized my attention.

Given the haste of our departure, our bags had been packed in a rush. Each of the children, even Leila, stumbled under the weight of a mixed assortment of bags, baskets and suitcases. Among other things, I had entrusted Denis with a bulky, black leather briefcase. But no sooner had he found his seat than he realized he no longer had it. I dashed out with him, back to the waiting room. But no matter how hard we looked under every seat, the briefcase was nowhere to be seen. Had the cleaners thrown it out? We rummaged through the garbage. In vain. Had an employee or a dishonest passenger stolen it? When I asked to file a complaint with the director of the airport, I was told there was no time and I would miss my flight. It was true—Denis and I had barely time to get back in the plane before the crew closed the doors.

You will have a better idea of how I felt when I tell you that the briefcase contained all my albums, full of photographs of my parents, of my brothers, my sisters and myself at every age. My parents were passionately fond of photography, a faithful testimony to their social ascension. Their car driven by a chauffeur in khaki, drill livery, their ever-imposing houses and my mother's increasingly sumptuous jewels had all been captured on film. In *Tales from the Heart*, I describe one of the lost photos which remains engraved in my memory: 'My brothers and sisters all in a row. My father, sporting a moustache, dressed in an overcoat with a fur collar. My mother smiling with all her pearly-white teeth, her almond-shaped eyes squinting under her shiny, rabbit-skin fedora. Standing between her legs, skinny me, disfigured by that sulky, exasperated expression I was to cultivate until the end of my adolescence.'

I broke down. Africa was not content to reject me—it was stripping me. Not only was it taking my

man, it was also wiping out my past, my references.
It was destroying my identity.

I no longer existed.

*' . . . This Earth. This Realm. This England.'*
*Richard III*

If anyone had predicted that a few years later I would marry an Englishman and end up adoring his country, I would have taken it for a joke in very bad taste. Because when I landed in London I hated the city with all my might. The sun, a genuine lazybones, slept in late and rose after noon; when it deigned to appear, it hid behind heavy grey drapes. As early as four in the afternoon it turned as black as night and a penetrating chill began to freeze the soul.

I didn't like Ghana very much, possessed as it had been with a vulgar frenzy while I was there. Except for Ajumako, it never appears in my writing. Yet the separation was extremely cruel, as if I'd lost my mother for a second time. I began to hallucinate. Patches of sun floated under my eyelids, the smell of the light filled my nostrils. And I was in the courtyard of the fort at Cape Coast, under the windows of the Asantehene in Kumasi or having a drink on the

•

terrace of the Grand Hotel in Accra. I was scared of waking up, for then I would see once again only a mean London street stretch out as far as an Underground station bustling with commuters.

To say that I missed Kwame would be an euphemism. At that time there were no e-mails, no SMS, no texting, no Facebook, no Twitter. Even telephone calls were expensive and difficult. I wrote to him every day, or several times a day, attempting with the paucity of words to wrestle with my pain, to fill the void into which I had fallen. I would take my bulky missives to a post office where two silver-haired sisters sold licorice rolls and haberdasheries. They would make a face weighing my letters: 'It's quite heavy, honey. First class? It'll cost you a fortune.'

I was not the only one to agonize. Leila, who could not bear Adeeza's absence, refused to eat and clamoured for her day and night. Her plaintive little voice broke my already aching heart.

'Deeza! I want Deeza!'

The other children, including Aicha, were morose and lacklustre.

You may well ask why I landed up in England. It was not my choice. I refused to be sent back to Guinea, and since Ghanaian legislation didn't allow me to be deported to France, there was no other solution.

In England, my good Samaritans went by the name of Walter and Dorothy. Friends of Kwame, they were an unorthodox couple. Walter, effeminate like certain English aristocrats, was a reputed journalist who had written a great deal on Nigeria where he had lived for many years. One of his books in particular had predicted the war in Biafra which would break out in 1967 and bleed the region for years. Dorothy was dark, sensual and vivacious.

They came to pick us up at the airport and drove us to the house of a certain Mr Jimeta, a Nigerian diplomat, on leave in his home country. I had never seen such a neighbourhood—rows of identical brick houses, so similar one could be mistaken for another, no doubt roomy and comfortable inside but appearing terribly sad from the outside. Given their sense of humour, the English were the first to poke fun at this symmetry. A story goes that, home from work, a man sits down in his living room to watch *Coronation Street*, then moves over to the table and eats his dinner, his eyes glazed over by routine. It is only when he gets into bed that he realizes the woman he is about to make love to is not his wife. He had walked into the wrong house and not noticed anything amiss until then.

Opposite us lived an Indian lady, Mrs Pandit. Every afternoon, at four o'clock, she would cross the street for 'a nice cup of tea,' the brew which, like the Guinean quinquéliba, was a cure for everything. On each occasion she would take the opportunity to drum warnings into me: 'Be very careful! The English loathe and despise us!' Racism for her was an endless subject of conversation; she would go on about it for hours while my thoughts roamed elsewhere.

Walter and Dorothy owned an enormous house in Golders Green where they raised their five children in a most unconventional manner—they would walk around naked, for instance, and sometimes even make love in front of them. Although one might find fault with their methods of education, I remain eternally grateful to them. With the help of Esther, their Nigerian servant, within a few weeks they had got my children to smile again and play games, something I was absolutely unable to do. Thanks to them, this brutal transplantation had no devastating consequences. Leila stopped clamouring for Adeeza, and Denis went so far as to ask me politely when I had finished reading over and over again my mail: 'How is Mr Aidoo doing?'

On the recommendation of Walter, who had a lot of connections with the media, and after a brief interview with a group of journalists, I was hired on a comfortable salary by the prestigious British Broadcasting Corporation at Bush House for their Africa programmes. When Mr Jimeta came back from Nigeria, I was able to move into an flat situated in the pleasant, though somewhat rural, locality of Highgate. A job, an flat! Unknowingly, my life was getting back to normal.

•

Tired as I was, I strung up some Ghanaian wrappers on the windows of my new flat in lieu of curtains. Immediately I received a threatening letter from the managing agent along with a petition from the tenants, ordering to remove these rags which were detrimental to the value of the building. I was also accused of not placing my garbage bins in the recess provided and of scattering the corridors on my floor with stinking detritus. Although I didn't smoke, I was said to be responsible for the burns on the rugs and carpeting in the games room of which my children made a mess. My 'barbaric' music, whereas I listened virtually always to the classics, disturbed my neighbours. The managing agent was sadly obliged to start eviction proceedings.

Oddly enough, this unfair harassment aroused me from my apathy. England was not Ghana where anything was possible and permitted. Ever since the Magna Carta, the country had endowed itself with laws for protecting its citizens. I engaged a lawyer who prevented my eviction. The only concession was that I had to replace my brightly coloured wrappers with dark, wine-coloured curtains bought from Selfridges. Thereafter, my fellow tenants left me in peace. More truthfully, they avoided me like the plague. Nobody bade me 'good morning' or 'good evening'. Faces grew expressionless and conversations stopped when I entered the lift. On several occasions, my letterbox was vandalized and my mail thrown out.

Plus the awful stories the children brought back from school.

'Nobody wants to sit next to us!'

'They say we smell!'

'They call us monkeys!'

Leila would begin to scream as soon as we left the flat in the morning and continue all the way on our walk across Highgate Park.

No, life was not treating us well. Fortunately, my work infused me with energy. For the first time, I who loathed teaching, liked what I was doing. 'Journalism can take you where you want,' Jules Janin said, 'provided you can forget you were once a journalist.'

The programmes at Bush House were produced by a group of competent African journalists, including Joseph Sane from Senegal and François Itoua from Cameroon. We had to interest our listeners in certain aspects of English culture. And we had a lot to choose from, as 'Swinging London' was packed with artists of every sort, of every colour and every nationality. It was my first contact with the yet-to-be-named 'cultural diversity'. I interviewed novelists and poets from South Africa, with Alex La Guma and Dennis Brutus taking pride of place. I spent a dazzling evening with Wole Soyinka, some of whose plays I knew. (Our friendship dates back to that time, and was evident whenever we met, in particular when I was teaching at Harvard. When we discovered we were born the same year, we decided to call each other 'brother' and 'sister'.) The tidal wave of reggae music was about to sweep the world and in the jam-packed concert halls of Soho I sat shoulder to shoulder with fans of this new music. Dorothy and Walter's parties were also cosmopolitan events, their guests ranging from Indian caricaturists to Japanese dancers to Indonesian batik painters.

Jan Carew, the Guyanese novelist, had also lived in Ghana but our paths had never crossed. His novel *Moscow Is Not My Mecca* was the subject of every conversation. His passionate tirades reminded me of Cabral. 'The expression "African socialism" is nonsense!' he thundered amid a circle of sceptics. 'Socialism is a very exact political construction which aims at destroying privilege and sets its sight on a classless society. Traditional Africa operated solely on accepted differences and acknowledged inequalities.'

In September, I enrolled at the University of London for two classes on Africa: one on the history of colonialism, the other on sociology of development. Both of them bored me. In the mouth of those university professors, two leading lights no less (but counter-revolutionaries, the Guineans would have called them in contempt) Africa lost all its dynamism and vivacity; it became an inert and lifeless lump of matter that each shaped to his liking. It was then that I heard the argument, recently the subject of a violent debate in France, that the slave trade by the Arabs had in fact been more harmful for sub-Saharan Africa than the Atlantic slave trade.

Even then, I wasn't really convinced.

Disappointed by the university, I tried to enrol at the London School of Economics. Unfortunately, my level of studies at the time entitled me only to audit classes in the Developing Countries section. Oddly enough, these classes, often arid but based on facts, figures and statistics, better suited me and satisfied my quest for the truth. I bitterly regretted I was condemned to silence and not permitted a presentation.

I was itching to enrol in a class of English literature. But I had the good sense to realize that, given my busy routine, it would be impractical.

Meanwhile, at Bush House, I was given the unexpected honour of producing a weekly portrait of English society from my point of view. I remember one episode on how the English adored their pets, who they seem to distinctly prefer to their fellow countrymen.

I was invited over and over again to roundtables and conferences to give my opinion on African politics and culture. These took place at Africa House where, besides the conference rooms and the cinema, they also sold drapes, masks and pearl necklaces. What upset me was that my opinions displeased and even shocked my audiences. Once I had to confront a furious group of people because I had, jokingly I thought, declared that Africa had never considered me a daughter—at the most, a cousin behaving strangely. I realized, at my unfortunate expense, that certain subjects could only be broached with extreme seriousness—nobody would tolerate them being addressed with humour or irony. But for me, those were the only ways in which I could, without whining about my lot, describe experiences that had been so painful, so traumatic.

The general outcry that greeted my discourses in no way deterred me from speaking my mind. On the contrary—I stopped at nothing. At the same time, oddly enough, my reputation did suffer. Although that seemed to delight Walter and Dorothy; they would rub their hands with glee before each party, anticipating a stormy confrontation between one of their guests and me.

'You are a born provocateur.'

I couldn't believe it. Is the truth a provocation? It had slipped my mind ever since that birthday when I had told my mother what I thought of her.

I received an incredible number of visitors who came under the pretext of discussing Guinea and Ghana and the future of Africa, but in truth had come to hear me utter an ill-placed comment.

•

Ama Ata Aidoo, who hated England, came to spend a few days with me. She was back from Canada where Roger Genoud held an important teaching position at McGill University.

'They don't like Montreal,' she said. 'They miss Ghana.'

Like all of us. Roger had begun to suffer from the illness that would eventually carry him off and she was worried. 'He has these constant fevers—40 and more. Is it malaria that won't let go?'

The beloved playwright had transformed herself into a staunch feminist, and she gave a fascinating presentation at Africa House on the role of women in the development of Africa, a subject which hadn't yet been flogged to death.

Our discussions often took on the acrimony of genuine quarrels.

'Africa is neither impenetrable nor indecipherable, as you like to think!' she'd fume. 'It has rules, traditions and codes that are easy to understand. It's because you're looking for something else.'

'Such as?'

'A land that is a foil that would allow you to be what you dream of being. And on that level, nobody can help you.'

And today I think she may have been right.

One day, Denis Duerden, who managed a charity, introduced me to a young Guadeloupean called Daniel Maximin who was studying for his Masters degree. Our friendship deepened while we worked together for *Présence Africaine*. We shared the same admiration for Césaire, but in spite of that, we were often in disagreement. For him, Césaire was the 'nègre fondamental'. He made no allowances for my reservations and that finally I preferred Fanon.

It was around this time that an important, I should say, major, event occurred—I began to write. It all happened quite naturally. No mystical experience, no particular circumstance. One evening, after dinner, while the children were asleep, I reached out for the green Remington typewriter which I kept for years afterwards and on which I typed the two volumes of *Segu*. I began to type with one finger but not my usual interviews, articles and reports for Bush House. And it was as if a lance had pierced my side and released a teeming flow of memories, dreams, impressions and forgotten sensations. When I stopped, it was three in the morning. I reread what I had written with a certain apprehension. I had written about my mother, and my father whom I nicknamed the 'Mandingo marabout'. It was the first draft of *Heremakhonon*. I worked on it for years before I met Stanislas Adotevi (yet another Good Samaritan), in charge of the collection 'La Voix des Autres' at the 10/18 publishing house.

I was searching for something I was unable to find or name. Without being told or taught so, I sensed that the events of a story should be narrated through a filter of subjectivity which was defined by the writer's sensitivity. Roughly speaking, despite the range of narratives, it remains the same, book after book. It is the unchanging voice of the author, however hard the professors of literature strive to distinguish Narrator from Author. My students understood it full well and made it the subject of their research.

And what about Kwame in all that?—you may well ask.

He was always with me. Despite the torture of not being able to speak to each other, to kiss and touch each other, we had never been as close as during this period of separation. One day in a rage I burnt the ardent letters he wrote to me—and I regret that even today. There was nothing to antagonize us, neither children nor political opinions. In his correspondence, he swore over and over again that, once my name was cleared, I would return to Ghana; that he was working on it relentlessly. In the meantime, he begged me to get my life back in order. And there was no question about it: the children had absolutely to go back to Condé. Then he would deal with my divorce. In six months, he claimed, I would be free to marry him. Wouldn't I like to be called Madame Kwame Aidoo?

I, however, was convinced I would never see Accra again. The thought of Kwame had become like a religious belief in the afterlife. It represented hope. It gave me enough courage to get up at six in the morning in the dark, dress, then take the reluctant children to their school, put up with almost an hour's journey from Highgate to Bush House, work with my colleagues, pretend to enjoy myself at Walter's and Dorothy's trendy parties—in short, to trudge along the path of this gloomy and solitary existence.

But hope is not assurance, and I was no means certain to meet up with him again.

It was this state of mind, this morose and confused conviction that despite my relatively young age my love life was over, which explains a terrible decision I made.

When the children went back to school in September, a ray of sunshine broke through the leaden sky of England. Denis, the unloved, constantly rejected, became the inseparable friend of a boy called Ethan Bromberger. They exchanged comic books and single records. After class, they locked themselves up for hours in Denis's bedroom where the girls were not allowed to enter. On Saturdays, they climbed onto their bicycles and pedalled to Hampstead Heath. On Sundays, they joined in the activities of The Young Music Lovers Association.

•

Years later, Denis revealed to me that Ethan had been his first homosexual love. At the time, of course, although I was surprised at how close they had become, I didn't suspect anything. I was very fond of Ethan; he was serious and polite and had just lost his mother giving birth to his third little brother.

He was always reassuring me: 'I'm sure you'll get along wonderfully well with my father.'

So that we could get to know each other, he invited me for tea to his home. He was not mistaken. Like our sons, Aaron Bromberger and I immediately became close friends. He was a gynecologist who owned a clinic in a pretty Victorian house a few streets away. He was dark like a mulatto, and sombre, owing to the recent loss of his beloved Naomi.

He was not the first Jew I had rubbed shoulders with—I had numerous Jewish friends at the Lycée Fénelon. But the term did not mean much to me. Senghor had been taken prisoner by the Germans during the Second World War, and my brother had died in the camps. Nevertheless, I had never felt implicated by Nazi barbarism. I'm ashamed to confess that I had never read *The Diary of Anne Frank*, and the names of Primo Levi and Elie Wiesel were unknown to me. This was, however, the first time I met a militant Jew. And a whole chapter of history suddenly opened up before me: the concentration camps, the Final Solution, the birth of the State of Israel and the conflict with Palestine. I was immediately struck by the similarity between the destinies of the Jewish 'race' and the black 'race', both equally despised and tortured throughout the world. This similarity of fate was constantly to haunt me, and it finally found its meaningful expression in *I, Tituba: Black Witch of Salem*. Those who have read it know that it focuses on Tituba, the slave from Barbados, who was shipped to the Puritans in America and blamed for the collective hysteria of the witches of Salem.

In the United States, the deliberately provocative intention of the novel's parody and mockery was somewhat obscured by Angela Davis' fine introduction, a little too serious and solemn for my liking, emphasizing the silencing and exclusion from history of certain peoples and individuals. I, however, wishing to break with the image of an old hag, turned Tituba into an attractive black woman who, on meeting Hester Prynne in prison, the heroine of Nathaniel Hawthorne's *The Scarlet Letter*, confides that she has a craving for men and that she will never be made into a feminist. She then becomes the lover of her Jewish master, Benjamin Cohen d'Alvezedo, deformed and hunchbacked; and when they are in bed together, instead of exchanging tender words, they launch into a sinister tally of their people's suffering: slavery and corporal punishments in the plantations for the Blacks; pogroms and ghettoes for the Jews. In the end, they never manage to determine who have been the greater victim of crimes against humanity.

Today I am torn like many people between sympathy for the unfortunate Palestinians and the aggressive face Israel often assumes in order to defend itself. In my novel *En attendant la montée des eaux*, the character Fouad, introduced precisely to reflect these concerns, declares: 'I'm Palestinian. But it's an identity that frightens people. The term itself covers too much suffering, dispossession and humiliation. You need to be a Jean Genet to like us. Otherwise the world turns its back on us.'

Aaron and I often talked about ourselves. Since his parents had to flee Nazi Germany with the rise of Hitler, his father, an acclaimed concert pianist, had languished, giving wretched music lessons to a series of uninterested pupils. His mother started out as a housecleaner, although never at the homes of Jews! We also often recalled our long-lost loves, Naomi and Kwame, and shared the sad conviction that children, however much we cherish them, often ruin our happiness. That's how we came to discuss contraception, and he described to me an operation he performed in which he tied the Fallopian tubes.

I can never stress enough that all this occurred before the pill, the morning-after pill, all those inventions that protect women from unwanted pregnancies. When I was young, one of our major concerns was to make love without paying for the consequences. Soon I begged him to operate on me—I no longer wanted to procreate. But he categorically refused on the pretext that I was too young.

•

'How do you know you won't meet someone who not only will take on your children but also ask you to give him others?'

After months of begging, however, he surrendered.

The operation lasted an hour under general anesthesia. When I woke up, I felt terribly unhappy. Why had I mutilated myself in this way? So I would no longer feel a foetus kick inside me? So I would no longer have long silent chats with the little stranger in my womb? So I would no longer hug to my breast a blind, awkward newborn with its characteristic smell of hummus? So he or she would no longer suck greedily at my breast with a little lukewarm mouth? All the clichés of maternity that I had been fed in my youth—the Virgin with Child, the Pietà, baby Jesus— passed through my mind. The very next moment I heaved a sigh of relief. Over!—the fear and anguish after every sexual intercourse was over.

If I had had a man within reach, I would have dragged him onto me, guessing that love would now have a sweeter taste.

I was, however, not entirely out of the woods.

When I returned home after three or four days in hospital, I found an official letter from Ghana waiting for me. I unsealed it with trembling hands—it was signed by Kotoka and Afrifa. I had to read it over and over again in order to understand its meaning: my lawyer, Mr Kwame Aidoo, had furnished proof that my deportation from Ghana had been a mistake. It was evident I was not a spy. Moreover, I had been very badly treated by the Nkrumah regime. Consequently, I had been awarded the sum of 10,000 cedis by way of damages. (Needless to say, I never received a cent). I was free to return to Ghana whenever I liked.

How can I describe what I felt? At first, I felt no joy. On the contrary. I had the conviction that once again Africa had laid a trap for me worse than those it had set for me in the past. It was handing Kwame back to me whereas I was no longer a woman—I was an empty husk. A sham. How could I dare face him? If our life returned to normal, he would demand an heir. How would he react if he knew I could no longer satisfy him?

Then, finally, I was overcome with happiness. The devil take this quibbling! I was going to get my man back. I telephoned Dorothy and Walter only to have the news greeted coldly. Soon after, they rushed over to Highgate to dissuade me from leaving.

'You're starting to make a name for yourself in London. And then Ghana's done for,' Walter said. 'I bet you another coup will occur very soon.'

He was right. Another coup was to rock the country in 1972. Plus others in 1979, 1981, 1982 and 1983. Five military and three civil governments succeeded one after the other until Jerry Rawlings was legitimately elected in 1992.

•

'You won't be happy with Kwame,' Dorothy said. 'Too selfish. Too calculating. Too full of himself. And he's a confirmed womanizer.'

I knew deep down that Kwame was not, strictly speaking, faithful—he often went out alone in the evening, feminine voices called for him frequently over the phone. More seriously, in Ajumako, he had been married, following traditional custom, to a princess with whom he sometimes spent part of the night. Kwamina begged me to be wary of her as she could have me poisoned. Yet all that was of no importance to me. In my eyes, it only added to the uncommon charm of his personality. And I was convinced I occupied an exceptional place in his heart.

After a night of tossing and turning, I made up my mind: I would leave. But what should I do about the children? There was no question of taking them back with me to Ghana.

The next morning I made a series of wild attempts to try and solve the problem. I checked out the boarding schools in the Paris area which might admit Denis, even Sylvie-Anne. But each of them required a guardian who would be responsible for the young boarder not only during the school holidays but also on weekends. So I wrote to my sister Ena, who I had not heard from in years, begging her to help her poor nephew and niece for whom she had done so little. A few days later, the letter came back with 'address unknown' scrawled on it.

•

I rapidly consulted Gillette who said that Ena had joined her partner for his retirement on the shores of Lake Geneva. She also said that Jean had been appointed ambassador of Guinea to Liberia. She had remained in Conakry with the children and was terribly lonely because her father-in-law, whom she adored, had just died.

'Jean is taking Fatou with the Beautiful Eyes with him to Monrovia,' she specified bitterly. 'Apparently she now has herself called *Her Excellency.*'

Both our marriages, Gillette's with an African bourgeois, celebrated with great pomp, and mine with a penniless actor, totally unknown, had ended in failure. What a sad state of affairs! Gillette ended her letter begging me not to go back to Kwame. With her usual inclination to exaggerate, she claimed: 'That man will end up killing you!'

Since I was unable to solve the problem of my children, I hesitated between the joy of leaving and the depression of staying. In the meantime, Kwame, who could not understand my procrastination, dispatched genuine ultimatums, his final letter ending with: 'After so many trials and tribulations, our happiness is here to stay.'

For my last evening in London, I had dinner with Walter, Dorothy and one of their friends, playwright

Joan Littlewood whose *Oh, What a Lovely War*! was a huge success in London and had just been performed in Paris.

'Why don't you live in Paris?' Joan asked me, having been charmed by the French capital. 'Their social services are much better than ours. You and your children will be much better cared for.'

'Maryse doesn't do things like everyone else,' Walter cut in.

I was at a loss to explain myself. My relation to Paris was highly complex. For me, Paris was not the City of Light, the capital of the world, like it had been for my mother. It was, rather, the place where I had brutally discovered my difference, where I had discovered the 'lived experience of the black man' described by Fanon in *Black Skin, White Masks*.

When I was a teenager in the metro or on the bus, the Parisians would make rude comments right to my face: 'She's cute, the little Negress!'

The children would shiver in fright whenever I sat down beside them. 'Maman, the lady's face is all black!'

I was invited to dinner at a classmate's and her young nephew burst into terrified screams at the sight of me; they grew even more uncontrollable as I tried to approach him. It was only when I discovered Césaire that I developed a more positive attitude to these experiences and grew proud of my African origins.

•

Above all, I could never get over the consequences of my affair with Jean Dominique. It was in
Paris that I had been hurt and humiliated. I had
suffered in my heart and in my pride. I had been
made an outcast and a pariah.

•

*'Never Long, Nathaniel, to Taste the Waters of the Past'*

*André Gide*, The Fruits of the Earth

Faced with my dilemma, Walter and Dorothy offered to take care of Denis and Sylvie-Anne.

'For one year,' Dorothy specified. 'That will give you ample time to realize what sort of man Kwame is and come back here where we will welcome you with open arms. God! What a waste!'

Sylvie-Anne was delighted to stay in London. She adored Walter and Dorothy who spoilt her outrageously and she got along like a house on fire with one of their daughters, Haby, far better than with Aicha whose character was so different. Denis, however, visibly sulked, close to comparing his lot with that of his beloved Ethan who had lost his mother.

'I hope you'll be happy,' he repeated boldly.

Aaron Bromberger, inconsolable, blamed himself entirely.

•

'I was so wrong to give in to your entreaties and carry out that operation. I warned you it was irreversible. And now you're leaving for a new life.'

New life?

Kwame had really done an excellent job: I returned to Accra on 10 September 1967, a little over a year since the coup which had me deported. I was accompanied by Aicha and Leila who had just turned six and four, hoping that their tender age would melt Kwame's heart.

I realized that I had seriously miscalculated.

'Hello Mister Aidoo!' Aicha said maliciously, offering her cheek for a kiss.

He complied after a long hesitation. Then he looked up at me with a mixture of rage and pain. Looking back now from my old age, I realize that at that very moment I had dealt a fatal blow to the love he felt for me. He did not have Condé's tolerant nature to accept me as I was. He thought I was trying to force his hand and could not forgive my duplicity.

He didn't say a word while we drove across town. Trying to break that awkward silence, I asked him a few questions in a strained voice.

'Have they started to try the ministers?'

'Not yet.'

'Is Kodwo Addison still in prison?'

'Yes!'

After that I fell silent.

He lived in N'tiri, a new ostentatious neighbourhood with ultramodern villas, lapped by a muddy sea that the promoters had never managed to make sparkling blue. An armed private militia patrolled the beach because Accra, once so safe, had been transformed into a den of thieves. The press, no longer reduced to the CPP's single sheet, reeled off descriptions of the most brazen and spectacular burglaries perpetrated by gangs prepared to do anything. In broad daylight, houses were emptied of their contents while their owners were at work and the furniture carried off in removal trucks.

The next morning, holding Aicha and Leila by the hand, I toured the town but didn't recognize it. An indescribable sadness hung over it. Gone were the sounds of high life on the loudspeakers. Deserted were the bars where once men and women got drunk on akpeteshie or the local gin. Rare were the passers-by dotting the public squares. I walked over to the institute where I'd once taught. The trim brick building was deserted. A group of students stood gaping on the veranda. The new director, Asiédu, who had taught Spanish when Roger was director, stared at me in amazement.

'What are you doing here? Weren't you deported to Guinea?'

'That's all been settled. Where are the students?'

He shrugged.

'Gone! Nobody wants to study languages any more. It was one of Nkrumah's mad ideas. People want to be in professions that make money—commerce, management.'

At lunch, I asked Kwame: 'What is positive about the new regime?'

'Freedom of expression!' he replied pompously.

'Is that all?'

'What do you mean is that all?' he was outraged. 'We now have at least a dozen newspapers. There are countless opposition parties. Elections are scheduled for June.'

I was not convinced. On the television, game shows and insipid American series, such as the hugely popular *Bewitched,* had replaced the endless speeches by Nkrumah on the ravages of colonialism. Was that progress?

I kept my questions to myself since Kwame was in no mood to respond.

One week after we arrived, Adeeza tracked us down and turned up at lunchtime. She was married and pregnant. Her husband, an electrician, was out of a job since the large-scale construction works begun under Nkrumah had all been halted. Leila, who had not forgotten her, threw herself into her arms and showered her with passionate kisses, whispering in her ear a long list of troubles she had endured while abroad. I was dumbfounded, once again petrified with jealousy—Leila was never as tender as that with me. But then, what feelings could she have for a mother who dragged her from country to country, from house to house and who inflicted on her that loathsome digression in England? In short, a mother who had initiated her at such an early age to the terrible experiences of uprooting, exile and racism.

When Adeeza left, I took Leila into my arms. I wanted to beg her—to try and forgive me for all the wickedness I had caused although through no fault of my own. Obviously, she did not understand either the meaning of my tears or my disjointed words and was content to return my kisses somewhat impatiently.

All that did nothing to improve my mood. As you have guessed, this return was not at all how I had imagined it. Kwame went out evening after evening, shortly after downing his dinner. By the time he returned, late at night, I was asleep. As a result, we seldom made love. Perhaps it was better that way, since the precautionary measures he took each time made me feel so guilty that I was tempted to tell him the truth. In fact, we seldom saw each other. He now worked for a major Nigerian oil company and used his new responsibilities as an excuse to always be absent.

'Do you need anything?' he would ask, then disappear for days on end.

Once he didn't turn up for over a week. I was so worried I went to his practice, and was amazed at how important it had become. How times had changed! Two other lawyers were seated imposingly amid about a dozen employees, and they all stared at me curiously. I realized I must be the subject of a great deal of gossip.

What worried me most was my financial situation. Kwame deliberately pretended as if I did not have two children with me. I had no idea how I was going to pay for their school uniforms, their canteen and the school bus. I hadn't yet read the book that was to top my list of favourites, Virginia Woolf's *A Room of One's Own*. And yet I understood very quickly that a woman must never depend financially on a man.

After a great deal of hesitation, I went and knocked on the door of the Ghana Broadcasting Corporation where Mrs Attoh-Mills greeted me with open arms. She now occupied an important position and had heard my programmes from London which she found intelligent and humorous. 'But why are you back?' she exclaimed. 'Since we lost Nkrumah, the country's dying. When he was here, at least we had enough to eat and the country was overflowing with tourists from all over the world. Now it's a desert!'

I have heard the same lament in very different countries after a change of regime and a so-called revolution. It conveys the despair of our people who expect happiness and are constantly duped.

Mrs Atoh-Mills and I agreed that I would produce a weekly programme on cultural events for the other English-speaking countries. It turned out to be quite a trial, since absolutely nothing was going on in Ghana any longer. And I ended up resorting to portraits of musicians. Only music was moving on through the tough times; the writers and playwrights, once so numerous, had fallen silent.

It was during this second stay in Accra, so disappointing, that I began to write in a more 'professional' way although still not imagining that one day I would be published. I wrote for hours on end. Once Kwame was at work and the children at school, the day stretched out wide open before me. I would sit down with my faithful Remington and a pile of cheap paper on the first-floor balcony. I would also place a stack of long-playing records on Kwame's record player. Sophisticated for its time, it was capable of turning the records over so that I could hear both sides. Music encouraged my creativity by surrounding me with beauty. The oil of harmony that lubricated the rusty cogwheels of the intellect, it made me lapse into forgetting the chores of everyday life.

•

I had and still have difficulty devising dialogue. I wondered whether it would not be better do away with it entirely, something I decided to do in some of my novels. After endless attempts, I adopted a strategy in *Heremakhonon* that to me seemed apt for the ill-defined personality of Véronica, the heroine: keep only the questions, and replace the answers by an often confused interior monologue or stream of consciousness.

Despite everything, Kwame and I managed to share some moments that bordered on happiness.

I accompanied him sometimes to Ajumako. His father was dead and his sister, Kwamina, had died of a heart attack. His young brother, now enthroned, was in charge of the kingdom. Consequently, Kwame's only role was as member of the Council of Elders. We seldom left our room in the second courtyard of the royal palace. In the evening, we went to listen to musical concerts in the main square. Servants brought us traditional stools and, as the night air was cool, they wrapped our shoulders in thick stoles of animal skins. I would look up at the sky studded with stars and wish passionately that I could start my life again—emerge from my mother's womb holding a new hand of cards. If there was a god hiding behind this immense opacity, why was he denying me the simple happiness he had given to so many others? Why was he multiplying my trials and tribulations? Where did he intend taking me?

Once, Kwame invited me to spend a weekend in Lagos where one of his friends was getting married. But we never attended the wedding, nor did I see much of that chaotic city. Some gangs had committed a series of horrible crimes, and the soldiers had cordoned off entire neighbourhoods. Police cars rushed around, their sirens furiously renting the air. So we locked ourselves up in our five-star hotel by the sea and made love, nonstop, for forty-eight hours.

Next to the hotel was a small bookshop where I bought Wole Soyinka's latest plays. 'I met him in London!' I said somewhat nostalgically.

To my surprise, however, since oblivion gives our memories a facelift, my life in London returned again and again to haunt me.

Sometimes Kwame organized receptions that were attended by his serious colleagues from the Bar and their embroidered wives, his cousins, the Boadoo couple, still just as eccentric, flanked by Yasmina, Irina's young sister, a model and surprisingly aggressive towards me. These receptions had nothing in common with the noisy, good-natured house parties which I used to attend with Lina. Waiters in white livery walked around serving champagne and canapés. No *kente* cloth but Giorgio Armani suits in wild silk. No wrappers or head ties but dresses bought in Paris or London. None of the national languages but English spoken in the most polished accents. I would wonder whether I had come all that way to end up in a circle in which the Grands Nègres would have been gladly accepted. They were 'mimic men' as described by V. S. Naipaul and Indian scholar Homi Bhabha whose work I relished later when I taught in the US. The coup had been carried out so that they could holiday in Acapulco and buy Audi Quatros. Who still cared about the people? No one.

But had anyone ever cared about them? Hadn't Nkrumah wanted to transform the country into a mirror where, like Narcissus, he could gaze at his own reflection?

*Osagyefo never dies.*

*The End of the Affair*
*Graham Greene*

I sensed I was living on borrowed time. And that everything was about to end.

But when? And how?

I was clinging to sleep, knowing that to wake up would be to see a nightmare.

It was almost Christmas, and Accra was reverting to the cheerful, sparkling town I had once known. In front of Flagstaff House, a huge Christmas tree flown in from Canada had been erected. One evening, in front of a crowd roaring with pleasure, imitating a custom imported from America, a minister in a suit and tie and his wife in a gold lamé dress arrived for the illumination. Then a choir of schoolchildren sang German carols, ending up with 'O Tannenbaum'.

At home, I had decorated a branch of casuarinas which represented what my means would allow. Every day, before dinner, we would go and sing carols a cappella at the neighbours who would then serve

•

small glasses of eggnog and savoury biscuits. But my heart was not in it. I had intercepted a letter from Aicha to Father Christmas asking him for two airline tickets to bring back Denis and Sylvie-Anne to Ghana; otherwise, she explained, we would spend Christmas with Mummy and Mr Aidoo, which would be too miserable.

Dorothy had just written: Denis had quarrelled with Ethan and they were no longer on speaking terms.

What had gone wrong between children who used to adore each other?

In contrast with the prevailing mood of sadness, I relived the Christmases of my childhood, the warmth and conviviality of the holidays. My parents never invited anyone; they were amply content with their eight children. What's more, they didn't have any friends, especially my mother who I had seen go through life alone. Christmas was the only holiday when they conformed to the culinary tradition, and nothing was lacking. Neither the piles of glistening, purplish black pudding nor the ham encrusted with its crackling nor the pigeon peas and the *pakala* yams, as white, as the expression goes, as the teeth of a lovely Negress. Although my mother preferred champagne, my father downed many a glass of rum and always ended up singing 'Faro dans les bois' out of tune while my brothers doubled up with laughter. One night, when I was still too young to accompany the family to midnight Mass at the cathedral of Saint

Pierre and Saint Paul, they left me asleep in my little bedroom next to my parents'. For some reason I woke up. The surrounding silence seemed unusual; as a rule, the house was full of the sounds of my mother's music and my brothers' and sisters' quarrelling. I went into my parents' bedroom. It was empty. Burning with curiosity, I crept up the stairs to the second floor. I say crept because my height did not allow me to reach the light switches and I groped my way along in the dark. Since I was now convinced there was no one in the house, I went back down to the living room and curled up on the sofa. There my parents found me two hours later, wide awake and dry eyed.

'Weren't you afraid?' my mother repeated, showering me with kisses.

My father found it a pretext to use one of the grandiose words he loved: 'This girl is the opposite of nyctalopic,' he said.

And since nobody knew what the strange word meant, he explained: 'Nyctalopic means night-blind.'

I was far from those years, now assigned to house arrest in this inhospitable villa which I had never got used to, with my two girls treated as pariahs by the master of the house and the servants.

As for Ghana, it was suffocating in the new rags it had borrowed from abroad.

•

One afternoon, Mrs Attoh-Mills dragged me to her clairvoyant. Mrs Attoh-Mills was my only friend. Lovely as well as good-hearted, she took my lot very much to heart and forced me to confront reality. 'You're in a tight spot! I advise you to make the first move and leave before Kwame throws you and your children out,' she said to me over and over again. 'You have no idea what the men here are capable of. Here you are and you won't budge. You just won't budge!'

Perhaps if I had followed her advice I would have spared myself a wound that took years to heal. Looking back, I can now confess that my stay in England, as difficult as it was, had comprised a number of positive factors: I had made friends from all over the world; in numerous circles, I had aroused esteem and consideration. I couldn't see myself going back to Europe. Yet, wasn't it time to put an end to this African venture, packed with suffering? Shouldn't I make up my mind and now show my face elsewhere?

Whatever their names, dibias, marabouts, obeah-men or mediums, they are fundamentally essential to the societies of Africa and the diaspora. Not only are they meant to predict the future, they are also capable of thwarting the evil dealt by fate. Although I was naturally sceptical and refused to use their services, the same was not true of people around me. Eddie, an ardent adept of mediums, told me a story which inspired me to write a novella for the anthology *Dark Matters* published in America. When she lived in N'Zérékoré in Upper Guinea, all her jewels disappeared. She was particularly affected because they were family heirlooms: a gold bead necklace and choker given to her by her mother, a chain bracelet from her First Communion and a cameo brooch that belonged to her grandparents. She dashed to look up a marabout well known throughout the region.

'Don't you worry!' he advised. 'You'll get your jewels back in three days' time.'

He refused to accept her money and requested instead that she make a gift of his choosing to an orphanage. Three days later, as he had predicted, her box of jewels reappeared on the kitchen table. Alas! Overjoyed at this 'miracle' which she told to one and all, she forgot to make the prescribed gift. Within a week, her jewels had disappeared again. The marabout whom she had dashed back to refused to receive her.

Mrs Attoh-Mills, involved for the third time, I believe, in thorny divorce proceedings, needed advice virtually every day. Her clairvoyant, who she said was the best in Accra, lived in Achampong, a working-class neighbourhood with pavements full of potholes and piles of rubbish. His house, identified by a huge notice board, was situated at the back of a yard swarming with women and children. A frail little man with an emaciated face, he stared at me for a while with his oddly glazed eyes and then whispered something to Mrs Attoh-Mills.

•

'What did he say?' I asked.

'He asked whether you know you are about to go on a long journey.'

'A long journey?' I repeated, panicking for some unknown reason. 'Does he mean I'm going to die?'

Mrs Attoh-Mills translated my question, and the dibia explained what he 'saw'.

'No, it's not that,' she said. 'You have many years in front of you. It's just that you will soon be leaving the country.'

As I looked at him in amazement, he took down from a shelf a jar full of murky liquid in which black-ish roots were macerating and held it out for me.

'Drink a soup spoon of this three times a day,' Mrs Attoh-Mills ordered on his recommendation.

If I had drunk that decoction, would it have changed the course of my life?


I went back to N'tiri, to an empty house since Aicha and Leila had not yet returned from school. How much longer was all this going to last? Kwame made only brief appearances—to pick up a change of clothes, to pick up some files and to give the servants their money. I kept telling myself that we should have a serious talk. But I was scared and couldn't pluck up the courage.

One morning he turned up on the veranda where I had reluctantly settled down to write. I was hard

•

up for ideas at the time. Seeing him at that unexpected hour, I knew the moment had come. But before I could speak, he announced in a monotone voice, as if reciting from a text learnt by heart, that he had purchased three airline tickets for me and the children. Since his finances did not allow him to send us back to London, he had booked a one-way flight to Dakar. Dakar was a French-speaking city where he knew I had a lot of friends.

'I'm getting married,' he added.

'To whom?'

'To Yasmine, Irina's young sister.'

I should have guessed.

'You'll never be separated from your children,' he concluded in a pained voice. 'I've finally accepted it.'

My memory has mercifully erased most of what happened afterwards. I recall I had, once again, a number of farewell visits: Mrs Attoh-Mills, the faithful Adeeza, her husband and the Boadoo couple.

But I no longer remember how I left Ghana or how I arrived in Senegal.

**III**

*'We Must Try to Live'*
Paul Valéry, The Graveyard by the Sea

One morning I opened my eyes and found myself lying in bed on the second floor of a wooden house with a wraparound veranda, planted in the middle of a sea of groundnuts. The house belonged to Eddie Bokoum, no longer a midwife but a United Nations civil servant. Not only did she operate the Infant and Maternity Protection Centre with the help of two nurses, she also toured the surrounding villages in a dilapidated van for vaccination rounds and Nivaquine hand-outs. It was the pre-AIDS era and, consequently, there was no distribution of condoms.

'The United Nations work here is a drop in the ocean,' she said. 'The Senegalese government should set up a genuine public-health programme. But no one gives a damn!'

·

It was Christmas Eve.

Aicha and Leila had left early for the party organized by their tiny school at the end of the street.

It hadn't rained for months. The earth was cracked. The air smelt of burnt vegetation. From my bed I could sense the waves of sweltering heat. I got up, washed, hastily dressed and went downstairs to the kitchen where, as usual, Fatou, the little servant, was dozing. For the sake of the children, I did my best to cook a chicken stuffed with chestnuts. Eddie had driven to Thiès to buy from a Martinican caterer some crab pâté and black pudding made of pig's blood (a sacrilege in this Muslim country, although it celebrated Christmas). The celebration therefore could go ahead even though I did not have the heart, not in the slightest.

Late morning, everyone returned home. The girls first, then Eddie's van swept into the unsightly shack of corrugated iron that served as a garage. Presents were handed out. Besides the inevitable children's drawings I received a bottle of Shalimar perfume by Guerlain. Eddie insisted on giving it to me. I knew she meant to say: 'Don't give up. You'll make a new life for yourself.'

I was on the verge of tears. What would I do without her?

Around seven in the evening, we left the girls in the hands of the old herniated watchman (with the red fez and who appears in all my books) and set off for church. Mass was no longer held at midnight, for this small town had become as violent as the rest of the world and hooligans took advantage of the owners' absences to ransack their homes. As night fell, a crowd of men and women walked towards the square concrete edifice topped by a cross. A Christmas crib had been set up at the entrance. The ox and the donkey, practically life size, watched over the pink-cheeked and blue-eyed baby doll.

'Couldn't they have found a black doll?' I kept thinking. Oblivious of this example of poor taste, the churchgoers made their offering in large jugs placed for just this purpose. Father Koffi-Tessio, a Togolese, was very proud of his choir. And with good reason, for that choir of 'pagan voices', as Senghor would say, sang beautifully the miracle of the Nativity.

I was really only there to please Eddie, since I hadn't set foot in a church for years. But I was amazed to hear myself sing the words of the hymns without fumbling, proving that I had not managed to fully eradicate a part of myself. Not only that: it kept coming back to haunt me. When it was time to take Communion, I felt the absurd desire to mingle with the human tide that surged up to the altar.

In a manner of speaking I loved Khombole. After my tumultuous years, it was as if I was back in the serenity of my mother's womb. And Eddie pampered me so.

•

'You frightened me,' she said. 'One day you asked me in earnest whether you'd be better off sticking your head in an oven like that English poetess.'

'American!' I corrected her automatically. 'Sylvia Plath was American.'

But this impression of being in a safe place was an illusion. Even in Khombole, adversity did not spare me. It was there, aghast and speechless, that Eddie and I learnt that our dear friend Yvane had died of cancer in the span of just a few weeks. At the same time, Gillette wrote that Jean had been brutally recalled from his post as ambassador. Accused of conspiring with foreign powers, he had been thrown into the Boiro concentration camp. Who knows if he'd ever get out?

In fact, we were never to see him again. Beaten to death, he had been buried in a common grave which Gillette never managed to identify. She spent the rest of her life in Guinea—she never wanted to leave out of fidelity to her husband. I borrowed her words for Rosélie when she says in *The Story of the Cannibal Woman*: 'My country is where he lies.'

As soon as I regained my strength, I sat down at my typewriter. Unknowingly, something had unlocked itself in me, and I was determined to be a writer. Like Roger Dorsinville, I blackened page upon page. I don't know how I came to such a decision. Of course

I had doubts; at times, I even thought it absurd that I was planning to feed four children with the smoke signals sent up by my thoughts. At other times, it seemed an arrogant assumption. Who was I to dare penetrate the magic circle of writers I admired?

On the whole, I stood my ground. What strikes me now is that I never thought of speaking about my problems: for instance, of evoking the tsunami of a love affair that had recently shattered me. Was it out of a sense of decency? Or a higher ambition? Consequently, before these memoirs, I have never talked about Kwame. He appears in some of my texts but almost behind a mask; I merely attribute some of his traits to my characters: his machismo, his arrogance and his insensitivity. On the other hand, as the years went by, certain political episodes continued to haunt me, such as the teachers' plot in Guinea to which I have referred time and again.

Eddie was one of the few people who keenly encouraged me to write. She was not satisfied, however, with what she read.

'If you write about everything you've seen, everything we've seen, you're bound to interest the readers! You philosophize too much! You make too many personal considerations. Tell us what you've seen! That's all. Period.'

On 6 January, it was Epiphany, I drove to Dakar in a run-down rental car to fetch Denis. Dorothy had mysteriously written to me that Denis could no longer stay with them for he had been extremely rude to Walter. She refused to say any more. It was Sylvie-Anne who told me: Denis had called Walter a 'dirty faggot' because he walked around naked in front of his children.

When Denis appeared in the arrival hall at Yoff Airport, he graced me with one of his radiant smiles, so much like his father's and which, alas, were to become fewer and fewer. His height caught my attention, for he was already almost a teenager and I no longer had to bend to kiss him. Although I had lectured myself on the way to the airport, I couldn't help bursting into tears: 'Please don't be angry with me! Don't be angry with me!'

He put his manly arms around my shoulders and hugged me: 'Be angry?' he exclaimed. 'How could I be angry with you? About what? If someone has suffered, it's you! I love you, Maman!'

I have kept Denis's words 'I love you, Maman!' deep in my heart through all these years of tension, confrontation, conflict and the all-too-short periods of reconciliation until the day he died, so cruelly, so unfairly, from AIDS in 1997. He was forty-one. He had written three promising novels. He was going to become a writer. He was the only one of my children who was interested in literature.

•

When I had more or less got my family together again, I thought it time to leave Eddie. I felt I had overstayed her generosity. I decided to settle in Dakar. There I again met cherished friends such as Sembène Ousmane, whom Senghor's authorities openly hounded and who was shooting his first feature film *La Noire de . . .* I accompanied him to the villages where, thanks to his connections, he managed to show his previous two films. Every time he turned up, it was reason for the villages to celebrate. We would wait for the night to bathe the main square before starting the projection. In front of the giant screen, the villagers sat on mats, some on the ground. Waiting for the first images to appear, the elders chewed venerably on their toothpicks. The children, seated on the ground in the first row, remained on their best behaviour. First the griots chanted, accompanied by the balafon. The acrobats juggled and somersaulted. Then silence fell. When the projection was over, there followed a discussion moderated by a young teacher from a neighbouring college. Sembène, in his generosity, never tired of answering all the questions. As usual, I didn't understand a word since all the exchanges took place in Wolof, the lingua franca. Yet I felt at home there amid the opacity of the night, wrapped in the warmth and conviviality of all these people.

I was also so happy to see Roger Dorsinville again. We had remained in touch and he knew all about my sentimental setbacks. Like Jean Brière, he predicted that Duvalier, now weary and worth millions, would soon retire as president and entrust the governance of the country to his obese son, Jean-Claude.

'He's mentally retarded!' Roger claimed. 'An idiot! Everyone knows it. Haiti is something out of Shakespeare.'

I experienced a pang of anguish when he told me about a journalist he considered one of the country's great hopes, a champion of the oppressed, a man called Jean Dominique.

'He's a mulatto,' explained Jean Brière. 'You know how colour counts for so much in our country. But he has made a complete break with the prejudice of his caste.'

'I know him!' I wanted to scream, 'He's a bastard! He wrecked my life!'

Subsequently, I often found myself in circles where the militants extolled Jean Dominique's merits: his exile in Nicaragua, in the US, his support for Aristide which turned into fierce opposition once the former priest became a dictator like all the rest, and, finally, his assassination, all of which made him a role model.

I did my best to keep my enraged thoughts to myself.

Only in 2003 did I lose patience, when Jonathan Demme's film *The Agronomist* was acclaimed by the left-wing press. My daughters rushed to the cinema to see for themselves the father of their brother and, afterwards, under his spell, wanted to know whether I had genuinely realized Jean Dominique's political stature.

Exasperated, I sent an open letter to a well-known daily where I had often published in the 'Opinions' section. I maintained that a man whose behaviour towards women was reprehensible could not be hailed as a hero. One or two days later, the chief editor called me, rather embarrassed, to tell me that the paper would not publish my letter for the facts that I described were a private matter. If he did so, he might very well be prosecuted for slander.

'If you want revenge, write a book!'

I was stupefied. For me a book is not a way to take revenge on someone, nor on life itself. Literature is where I express my fears and my anguish, where I attempt to free myself from my obsessive questioning. For example, when I wrote *Victoire, My Mother's Mother*, the most painful book I have written, I endeavoured to solve the enigmatic character of my mother. Why did a woman, genuinely good, generous and sensitive, behave so disagreeably? She constantly let fly poisoned arrows at everyone around her. By way of introspection and while writing the book, I was able to understand that her complex relationship with her mother was the cause of this contradiction: she had always been ashamed of the illiterate mother she adored, and she constantly blamed herself for being a 'bad daughter'.

•

Roger Dorsinville was the first person to read the complete version of *Heremakhonon*. Two days later he gave me his verdict.

'So much turgescence! Aren't you afraid of being mistaken for your heroine Véronica Mercier?'

I looked at him amazed.

I had no idea he would be right.

When the novel was published in 1976, journalists and readers were quick to believe that Maryse Condé and Véronica Mercier were one and the same person. They heaped criticism on me. They even went so far as to blame me for her amorality and chronic lack of willpower. I discovered that the writer, especially if she's a woman, should only portray paragons of virtue so as to safeguard her reputation.

I also saw Anne (now Arundel) again. In a trunk she thought contained a lot of worthless stuff she had discovered some exercise books full of Néné Khaly's poems and was trying to get them published. She had already sent them to a dozen publishers, but in vain.

'You understand, they're too revolutionary,' she claimed. 'They're dynamite.'

Anne Arundel did not like *Heremakhonon* at all, but for different reasons.

'That's not at all how it happened,' she blamed me.

For her, like for most people, literature has little more merit than a photograph, a certified copy of life. They are unaware of the considerable role played by the imagination. My teachers' plot was not the conspiracy we experienced. In *Heremakhonon*, I have piled together memories of my brief encounter with Mwalimwana-Sékou Touré at the Presidency, the behaviour of the students at the Bellevue college and my own terrified feelings during the coup d'état in Accra.

At this juncture, since Anne's mother had died, she settled in Noirmoutier and never got in touch again. Literature and friendship don't get on well together. To my knowledge, Néné Khaly's poems have never been published. Were they too violent? Was Anne right after all?

An ad in the Dakar daily *Le Soleil* announced that a newly created International Development Institute was hiring translators. In light of my experience in Ghana, I was easily recruited. The salary, aligned with that of the international civil servants, seemed excessive given the population's general state of poverty. But I didn't complain. It allowed me to buy a dark red Peugeot 404. I started driving again at breakneck speed, and moved into a huge villa in the Point E district, a residential and bourgeois neighbourhood.

In the villa next to ours lived Madame Bâ, a generous and motherly woman, as different from me as

•

could be. The wife of a lawyer, she herself was uneducated since she had married very young and spent her time giving birth to her children. Twelve in all. To me she was the mother I was incapable of being, maternity at its noblest.

'Being a mother,' she would repeat, 'is a full-time job. You can't afford to do anything else.'

Listening to her, I was increasingly ashamed of my separation with Condé, of my moving from one country to the next and of my lovers who refused to play the role of father. I admired her. I also suffered from the way my children adored her. Denis called her 'super-maman'.

At work, however, disappointments began to mount. At the institute, I soon antagonized everyone. I have already said I have no interest in translation. I began therefore by quarrelling with the corrector, a fussy old Frenchman tired of rewriting my texts. Furthermore, my colleagues complained of my constant lateness, my absences and of what they called, rightly or wrongly, my impoliteness and superior airs. In short, my three-month trial contract was not renewed. I did not suffer unduly since I wouldn't let one more humiliation stop me. Yet I had to feed all these mouths and couldn't go on borrowing money from Madame Bâ or Eddie. I thought it wise, therefore, to go back to teaching. I didn't like it either but at least I did it adequately.

I was hired without difficulty at the Lycée Charles de Gaulle in Saint Louis du Sénégal.

Unfortunately, since the Senegalese public-sector salaries were laughable, I would be unable to make ends meet. Eddie advised me to try and obtain a contract with the French Ministry of Overseas Development which paid far better. This meant that I would have to re-endorse my French nationality. I started by refusing. Although my Guinean passport had caused me nothing but problems, I had considered it a symbol of my freedom and my independence from the Grands Nègres.

In the end, I followed Eddie's advice as I had no intention of suffering again the all-too-familiar financial difficulties. Alas, I had not foreseen the endless visits to the French Embassy, the humiliations inflicted by the petty, obtuse and racist staff, as Eddie put it, and the number of times I had to explain my situation.

'If you were born in Guadeloupe, why have you got this passport?'

'It was given to me when I married a Guinean.'

'Did you ever renounce your French nationality in writing?'

'No!'

'Prove it.'

I was on the point of giving up when Sékou Kaba miraculously sent me the precious 'Certificate of Non-Repudiation of French Nationality' that was required.

•

I initialled my brand-new documents and felt like a failure.

Mid-September, Sylvie-Anne returned from London. She spoke only English. Unlike Denis who refused to talk about his stay in England, Sylvie-Anne was bursting with wonderful stories about her life with Walter and Dorothy. She was the princess and called her little sisters, Aicha especially, ignorant 'nitwits'. Her relations with Aicha, always difficult, now became truly hostile, with quarrels over the slightest thing. I endeavoured to consider the tension as an expression of the inevitable rivalry between sisters of a similar age. Nevertheless, it hurt me to see my dear daughters tear themselves to pieces.

With an aching heart, I made my farewells to Madame Bâ, returned my villa to its owner and sold my lovely car. Then we caught the train to Saint-Louis. I must confess that deep down, since I'd left Kwame, I had been feeling increasingly burdened— by the life I was leading, by the responsibility towards my children. I couldn't shake off the idea that I was the victim of an unspeakable injustice. Why was fate dealing me this spate of misfortune? I became irritable, aggressive and torn between con-tradictory feelings.

'What's the matter with you?' Eddie would com-plain. 'You're becoming unbearable.'

The train to Saint-Louis meant an entire day spent in an uncomfortable and sweltering carriage. The poverty of the villages we passed was stupefying. Was Guinea worse than this? At each stop, in spite of the whiplashes generously dealt by the guards, beggars took the train by storm and left behind a terrible smell. It was like witnessing the worst hours of colonialism.

Saint-Louis, the town of the 'signares', the women of mixed blood married to Frenchmen, had a charm of its own. It reminded me of France Zobda's interpretation in the beautiful *Les Caprices d'un Fleuve* released in 1996 with Bernard Giraudeau in the main role. I loved that old-fashioned town, unlike any of the places I had, or have, lived in. In the evening, walking with the children under a reddish, golden sky, I would sometimes wander as far as the district of N'Dar Toute. The peace of the place would creep over me and I would be gripped with a stubborn hope. I would be certain that the torment of my life was about to subside and at last I would be at peace with myself.

Yet, despite appearances, Saint-Louis was a town of petty squabbling. The Lycée Charles de Gaulle was a huge barrack-like building, housing hundreds of pupils from all the surrounding villages. The teaching staff was largely composed of French nationals openly come to 'make money'. They were nicknamed 'white trash' and Jean Chatenet predicted in his best-seller that 'one day they would all be eaten.' They made no effort to hide their contempt for the local personnel, the Africans who were paid three times less for the same work, not only because of their colour but also because of their allegedly inferior diplomas.

There was also a handful of Antilleans in the group married to French women. I recognized a mulatto, a certain Harry, married to a voluptuous blonde who had been in school with me at the Lycée Carnot in Pointe-à-Pitre. He ignored me superbly, obviously wanting to hide his origins. Years later, when I came back to live in Guadeloupe, I found myself seated next to him during a dinner at friends'. I reminded him jokingly of his attitude at that time. He defended himself brilliantly: 'It's because you frightened everyone. You were devilishly disagreeable. Nobody knew where you came from. Were you English-speaking? Were you French-speaking? You didn't have a husband but dragged around a flock of children of every colour.'

Of every colour? He was exaggerating. Only Denis was of mixed blood.

The staff room symbolized the civil war between the two factions of teachers. The French sat on comfortable seats along the windows while the Africans sat wherever they could. The French laughed, conversed in loud voices, cracked jokes. The Africans stayed silent or whispered in their language. Perhaps for the reasons outlined by Harry, I was ignored by everyone. I remained standing in a corner, waiting for the bell to ring and announce the start of classes. Too poor to pay for even a bicycle, I walked across the Faidherbe Bridge four times a day like my African colleagues who were as broke as I was. In contrast, the French drove by at the wheel of their cars without a glance in our direction. My heart swelled with bitterness. The fact, however, that I was rejected by both the French and the African teachers led me to look for acquaintances outside their circle. And through my daughters I was introduced to the Moroccan community.

Saint-Louis is home to a large community of Moroccans, a legacy of the merchants who settled there at the time of Faidherbe. We were invited to join in the feast of Eid-al Fitre, and, every weekend afterwards, to share in a barbecue of roast sheep or couscous. Seated on the mats in the midst of a dozen guests joking noisily, I learnt to eat with my hand, something I had always refused to do in Guinea. I sipped my four glasses of mint tea. At these meals, the role of the women was reduced to serving the succulent dishes they had spent hours preparing. Nevertheless, their radiant smiles warmed my heart and I understood at last that feelings are not necessarily expressed through words.

It was during one of these meals that I met the man who was to cure my solitude. Mohammed worked with his older brother, Mansour. Now over thirty years old, I had never known what Sartre and Beauvoir called a 'contingent' love; my love affairs

•

had always been violent dramas. Mohammed was young and his smile was as radiant and appealing as an adolescent's. When I realized what he wanted, I was stupefied. I had just been so humiliated and hurt that I wondered whether I was still a woman capable of seducing and arousing desire. I threw myself passionately therefore into this new type of relationship. I rediscovered physical satisfaction—I had forgotten the taste of kisses and embraces. I experienced the delicious feeling of being cared for and protected. Mohammed was extremely attentive. He owned a Renault 4L and put himself entirely at my disposal. From that moment on I no longer needed to cross the Faidherbe Bridge on foot, sweating under the sun, four times a day. I no longer came back from the market weighed down by my baskets.

Mohammed was also always ready to serve as a guide. We visited the region around Saint-Louis. We drove as far as Richard Toll on the border with Mauritania. An experimental garden had been created in the nineteenth century on the banks of the river Sénégal by French botanist Jean-Michel Claude Richard. Richard had introduced over three thousand plants, now commonplace, such as banana, cassava, orange, sugar cane and coffee.

Very soon this relative well-being was overshadowed by Denis. On the rare occasions when he emerged from his sulks and deigned to address Mohammed, he would poke fun at him, be contemptuous, almost rude. It was a fact that Mohammed, who was accountant for Mansour, a merchant dealing in salt and dates, was not very educated. It suited me perfectly. I had been so cruelly stung by an 'intellectual' that I had a grudge against the entire species. Mohammed entertained me and made me dream as he recounted his adventures in Fez, Marrakech and Istanbul: kasbahs, souks, palaces with azulejo-covered walls and century-old mosques. Denis, who had begun to demonstrate his superior intelligence and his execrable character, showered him with mean questions which poor Mohammed couldn't answer. For example, regarding the sultan of Morocco's exile to Corsica, then Madagascar and the reasons for his return home and his relations with the French.

'I don't hold it against him!' Mohammed assured me. 'He's jealous. I went through the same when my mother divorced my father who beat her and cheated on her with the servants under her nose. I couldn't bear the man she remarried.'

As a result, he made every effort to be gentle while Denis made every effort to be insolent. One day when Denis had been especially loathsome, I confronted him about his behaviour.

'He's not worthy of you!' he hissed. 'He's good for nothing.'

'What do you know to claim such a thing?' I said softly.

However hard I insisted, he wouldn't say another word.

On the second floor of our building lived four young English girls and one Irish girl with flaming red hair. They were members of the United Nations Association and taught in elementary schools. Very soon we became friends. Not only had we spent over a year in London but also for my daughters, Sylvie-Anne especially (since Denis had never managed to master it), English remained their only real language. We often got together for tea with scones and muffins. They loved Africa, for them a land of deprived children whom they dreamed of pampering. They invited them for tea and taught them games and nursery rhymes such as:

Ba, ba, black sheep
Have you any wool?
Yes, sir. Yes, sir.
Three bags full.

I was particularly friendly with Anne, the Irish girl. We went on long walks together and she told me wistfully of her boyfriend, Richard Philcox, who was a teacher in Kaolack, too far away.

In Saint-Louis, we were not totally lacking in artistic entertainment. We attended numerous open-air concerts of traditional music. The great Haitian actors, friends of Roger Dorsinville, Jacqueline and Lucien Lemoine, came to perform a play by Bernard Dadié, an author from the Ivory Coast, in the city hall. In order to celebrate the Fourth of July, the American cultural services screened *Gone with the Wind* which I enjoyed watching again. Although the

•

girls were transported by the story's torrid romanticism, Denis denounced the paltry image of the Blacks in the film, accentuated by inept dubbing. I was overjoyed to see him so critical, so lucid and articulate while predicting the problems his attitude would later raise.

In short, a life of imperfect, unpretentious happiness trundled along.

My writing projects, however, were by no means forgotten. Very often, I refused to spend the night with Mohammed who could not understand why I preferred to lock myself up with a typewriter. But I was constantly correcting what was to become my novel *Heremakhonon*. Without knowing it, the text had changed in nature—it was no longer a simple story inspired by my experiences. I had become more ambitious—I had started to erase the particulars which would have connected my characters to human and identifiable models. I now intended giving Véronica's choice a wider symbolic significance. Ibrahima Sory, the 'Nigger with ancestors', and Saliou, the militant, became the symbols of two warring factions of Africa: the dictators and the patriots. In other words, Sékou Touré versus Amílcar Cabral. Such a motive explains the phrase I have often been blamed for because it has been misunderstood, when Véronica, Ibrahima Sory's mistress, says:

'I looked for myself in the wrong place. In the arms of an assassin.'

Having learnt that Ellen Wright, Richard's widow, whom I had met frequently at the Genouds' in Accra, was now a literary agent in Paris, I moved heaven and earth to obtain her address. I wanted her to read my manuscript. And, if she agreed, to suggest an editor. But when I found her address I was so petrified that I was unable to make a move.

Mariama Bâ told me that she would never have published *So Long a Letter* if relatives working at the Nouvelles Editions Africaines publishers had not taken matters in hand. I'm convinced that if my friend Stanislas Adotevi had not forced my hand, *Hermakhonon* too would not have seen the light of day. (Stanislas Adotevi, director of the 10/18 collection 'La Voix des Autres' published by Christian Bourgois, had become infatuated with the novel.)

It was then that I received an official letter. I had learnt to be suspicious of those heavy brown envelopes. They were an ominous sign. The first one had launched me upon my career in Africa. The second had expelled me from Winneba. The third had requested me to return to Ghana and set off a series of disastrous consequences. This one was from the French Ministry of Overseas Development telling me that my application had been accepted. The problem was that I was posted to the Lycée Gaston Berger in Kaolack, in the Sine Saloum region. I was to take up the position on 5 January.

My first reaction was to refuse. To accept it implied leaving Mohammed, but above all it meant perpetuating the never-ending cycle of displacement and uprooting. Once again my children would lose their friends and their routine would be turned upside down. Nevertheless, could I remain insensitive to the fact that the salary on offer was three times the one I was currently being paid?

Mohammed and my Moroccan friends did their very best to discourage me. According to them, Kaolack was a horrible hole, riddled with flies and disease, the hottest point in Sénégal. The temperature averaged 45 degrees Celsius day and night. The fluorine in the water blackened the children's teeth.

Anne, the Irish girl, thought it decidedly unfair. Why wasn't she posted to Kaolack?

Finally, Mohammed borrowed his brother's van, piled in children and baggage and drove the almost 300 kilometres that separated us from Kaolack. I was heartbroken. It was not yet daylight and the little town of Saint-Louis was still asleep. A few fruit and vegetable sellers were pushing their carts along the Faidherbe Bridge, still drowned in mist.

It was to be one of my last trips in Africa.

What did tomorrow have in store for me?

We arrived in Kaolack early afternoon and were aghast. Flies everywhere. They settled on our lips, on our eyes and cheeks and crept into our nostrils. The heat exceeded anything I had known and soon our clothes stuck to our bodies. The housing agency had allocated me a string of dark, airless rooms above a grilled-meat seller.

I enrolled the girls in a series of prefabricated huts which served as an elementary school and where Sylvie-Anne swore quite openly she would never set foot.

It was a pleasant surprise to discover that the simple meal of roast chicken and potatoes served at the Hotel de Paris was quite good. Two French women at the next table took an interest in the girls: 'They're so cute,' they said. 'Are they all yours?'

Drawing up their chairs they came to sit at our table for coffee. They were both doctors working for the WHO.

'You'll see, it's not as bad as it seems!' they reassured me. 'We're not too far from Dakar or Bathurst in the Gambia which is a pleasant little town. What's more, the region is interesting—for example, there's the salt works. And yes, we know, it's hot!'

There remained, however, the last station of my cross. Once dinner was over, we retired to our room on the second floor of the Hotel de Paris and Mohammed stretched out on the bed. Quite casually he informed me that he was getting married the next

•

week. What! Was I condemned to live over and over again the same scene? In answer to my violent reaction, he assured me that it would not change a thing between us.

'I'm marrying Rachida to please Mansour and the family. I don't feel anything for her. We'll have children. Lots of boys, especially.'

I thought the cynicism of such a declaration to be the supreme insult not only to me but also to the girl he was about to marry. At eleven o'clock that evening, I threw Mohammed out into the corridor.

That was the last time I wept because of a man.

I woke up the next morning without the slightest premonition. The weather was overcast and sultry as was usual in Kaolack. The flies were already way onto everything. I drove my children to school, drying their tears as best I could. Then I went to report at the Lycée Gaston Berger, a long, shapeless building. The staff room hummed like a hive. Unlike the Lycée Charles de Gaulle where most of the teachers were expats, the majority here were African except for a trio of white youngsters sitting alone at a table. On seeing me, one of them got up and quickly came over: 'Are you Maryse? I'm Richard,' he said in French with a strong English accent.

He was Anne's boyfriend whom she had thoughtfully notified of my arrival in Kaolack. He was handsome, very handsome even, with large brown eyes in a suntanned face. I confess that this untimely familiarity shocked me coming from a complete stranger, looking so young, certainly younger than I was. Then I thought that this young English speaker was struggling as is often the case with the complexity of the French language.

I didn't realize that he was establishing a bond of intimacy between us. He was the one who was going to change my life. He would take me back to Europe, then Guadeloupe. We would discover America together. He would help me gently let go of my children while I resumed my studies.

Above all, thanks to him, I would begin my career as a writer.

Africa, finally subdued, would transform itself and slip, domesticated, into the folds of my imagination and be nothing more than the subject of numerous narratives.